“For a Christian, discovering the journey and often times a mystery. In *Because You're Called*, Jeff Maness clearly helps us understand our unique calling and then challenges us to live out our calling. Jeff doesn't just write about this stuff, he lives it. Jeff's life is completely motivated by the calling God has placed on his life. In addition, God is using him to do *great* things for the Kingdom because he is obedient to *the call*!”

Dr. Eddy Shigley
Founder and President of Doulos Leadership Group, Inc.

“Many people wrestle with their calling in life. Every person wants to make a difference, to effect positive change in the life of others, and to matter. This is why I am so excited that my friend, Pastor Jeff Maness, has written Because You're Called. Jeff is a fantastic communicator who has committed his life to helping others see their potential as God sees it. I'm praying this book will help you more clearly understand your unique calling and challenges you to take action!”

Joe Sangl
Founder and President of I Was Broke, Now I'm Not and Owner and President of Injoy Stewardship Solutions

"But forget all that --- it is nothing compared to what I'm going to do. For I am about to do a *brand-new thing*. See, I have already begun! Do you not see it? I will make a pathway in the wilderness for my people to come home. I will create rivers for them in the desert."

(Isaiah 43:18-19 NLT 1st edition)

BECAUSE YOU'RE CALLED:
Three words that will change your life

Jeff Maness

Lauren Grant Publishing Co.

Italics in Scripture quotations reflect the author's added emphasis.

ISBN 978-0-615-88305-2

Library of Congress Control Number: 2013916324

Cover design by Hayley Laban
Author photo by Jeremiah Karr

Printed in the United States by Morris Publishing®
3212 East Highway 30
Kearney, NE 68847
1-800-650-7888

CONTENTS

Acknowledgements

To Jesus: The fact that you saved me and changed my life is almost too much to bear. The fact that you chose me to lead my beautiful wife and four amazing children takes that to a whole new level. The fact that you called me to be a pastor of *Your* Bride…I don't even know what to say. Thank you for saving me. Thank you for changing. Thank you for choosing me. Thank you for calling me. That reality drives me to *You* every day.

To my wife: Sabrina, if I didn't have you in my life I could not be a pastor. I couldn't lead the way I lead, preach the way I preach, or pastor the way I pastor without you by my side. You are not behind me, you are *beside* me, and that makes all the difference in the world. If I could choose anyone to go on a vacation with, see a movie with, go to a ballgame with, or just hangout with, it will always be you! You are an amazing wife, the best mom, and *the* pastor's wife Element Church needs. Thank you for being yourself, for choosing me and for believing in me.

To my children: My goal as your dad is to lead and love you in a way that you will love Jesus and His church when you're my age. I'm so proud of each of you. Jonah my man; be as bold as a lion. (Proverbs 28:1) Mariah, my princess, Makalah, my Care Bear and Jaydah, my Jewel; you are unique, loved, chosen and strong…*live* in that reality! I love you and am so thankful God chose me to be your dad!

To my parents: Your dedication to God, commitment to each other, leadership of us kids, and love for the Church have made me into who I am today! If I can be half the parent you guys are I'll be an enormous success. Thank you for modeling to us the life of pursuing God's call…even when it was difficult!

To Joe Sangl: Thank you for pushing me to write a book. Without your encouragement and help this would not be a reality.

To my staff and volunteers: Betsy, thank you for your incredibly hard work, above and beyond your salary, to make sure this book was the best it could be. Kody and Dennis, thank you for supporting me and allowing me to pursue what God placed inside of me. Derek and Steve, thank you for allowing me to share the story of how God put a calling on your lives. Adam Cruz, while you weren't here with us while I wrote this book, I truly don't believe I would have written it without your partnership with me at Element. I am blessed with the best staff on the planet, and the greatest volunteers in the world, who have gone above and beyond to make this thing a reality. "Thank you!" hardly does it justice. I can't imagine being anywhere else or doing anything different than what I do right now with you. I love you guys!

To my mentors & coaches: Chris England, Dan Morgan, Tim Roehl, Eddy Shigley, Bryan Miles, you are all a part of my story. Thank you!

To Element Church: Without you, this book would not be a reality. God is fulfilling His promise through you. "Behold, I'm about to do a brand new thing!" That promise was not just for the *confirmation* of our church; it's for the *continuing* of it as well. God is doing brand new things through you. I take very seriously that God called me to be your pastor. I may not know each of you personally, but I love every one of you incredibly. Element, I hope to be your pastor until I retire or die! (Preferably the first) Buckle up church! The best is yet to come…because *we're* called!

FOREWORD

Many people wrestle with their calling in life. Every person wants to make a difference, to effect positive change in the life of others, and to matter. In our daily work, it can sometimes be difficult to see how our work fits into the will of God. Even more, if our work is not directly involved in ministry, we can feel as if our work is subordinate or less important. God's word is clear that our life and work matters to Him – and that each of us have a calling on our life.

I have encountered so many people who believe the lie that God is done with them or doesn't have a calling for their life. They feel completely lost. If this is you, I'm convinced this book will help you!

Here is what I know to be true: you are indeed called, you matter, and you are amazing! God has created you on purpose, with a purpose, and for a purpose. This is why I am so excited that my friend, Pastor Jeff Maness, has written *Because You're Called* – Three Words That Will Change Your Life. Jeff is a fantastic communicator who has committed his life to helping others see their potential as God sees it.

On a personal note, I have seen God use Pastor Jeff in an amazing way. He has sacrificed his personal dreams for God's preferred future. His commitment to reaching people for Jesus and to his family are driven by living the very words written in *Because You're Called.* As a result, God has exploded Element Church to become one of the fastest growing churches in the world, and it has happened in Cheyenne, Wyoming! Because Jeff was called – and responded – thousands of people's lives have been transformed forever. I'm praying this book will help you more clearly understand your unique calling and challenges you to take action!

Joseph Sangl

Joseph Sangl is the founder of I Was Broke. Now I'm Not., a ministry dedicated to helping people win with their money God's way. He is also the owner and president of INJOY Stewardship Solutions, a ministry dedicated to helping church leaders fund the God-given vision.

INTRODUCTION

Because You're Called: Three words that will change your life

I was on the way to the home of one of our staff members, who also happened to be one of my closest friends, to have the hardest conversation of my life. There was a pit in my stomach, my mind seemed to be in a million places and my heart felt like it was in a million pieces. The cost of what happened the day before was almost too much for me to bear. I felt like I was one step away from calling it quits. I loved the city we were in. I loved the church that I led. I loved the people I got to do life with, but I didn't know if it was worth it any longer. So I called the only person I knew who understood what we had been through…I called my wife.

She was one of the few people who even knew what had happened the day before, and she was the only person who knew what I was on the way to do. I don't think the phone call surprised her one bit. She answered with no other words but, "Hey!" I hesitated, felt a lump in my throat, and through some tears choked out, "Tell me why I'm doing this again." Her reply will forever echo in my heart. It's what kept me going that day, and it's what keeps me going every day. "Because you're called," she said. "Because you're called."

As I look at my life now, that one phrase has changed everything for me. Those three words have literally changed my life. People ask, "Why did you choose to become a pastor?" I always tell them in some form or fashion, "I didn't choose to be a pastor, God chose me. I'm a pastor because I'm called."

I can't tell you how many times I've been asked about Element Church: "Why Cheyenne? What made you choose Cheyenne, Wyoming?" And my answer has always been, "Because we were called."

My children have even been a part of this conversation. We have four kids, our oldest being our son Jonah. In the summer of 2006, the year we received God's call to start Element Church, he was five years old, and I'll never forget a conversation we had as we were driving down the road.

As best we could, my wife and I had explained to Jonah that we were leaving the only home he had ever known, the only friends he'd ever had, the only city he'd ever lived in and the only church he'd ever remembered to move to a new community; live in a new home, be forced to make new friends and to start a new church. It's hard enough to explain that to a 25 year old, let alone a 5 year old.

At the time of this conversation, Jonah had known about our new adventure for several months, but something was stirring in his heart and mind; you could just feel it. All of a sudden from the back seat of my pickup, buckled in to his car seat, Jonah asked, "Why isn't Zoe moving to Cheyenne?" (Zoe was one of Jonah's friends from the church) I did my best to explain why their family was staying and our family was going, to which he asked why a number of other friends and their families weren't going. He eventually got to the question he really wanted to know. "Why are *we* moving to Cheyenne?"

It's only the introduction of the book, but you probably already know the answer I gave. "Because we're called, Jonah. God called us to start a church in Cheyenne so that's what we are going to do." The follow up question from my 5 year old blew me away, and like the statement my wife made, will forever echo in my heart. "What if God called us to a place where there were wars?" Whoa! Can I just answer about Zoe again? That was way easier!

I paused…he waited…I paused a little more and said, "Well Jonah, I guess if God called us to a place where there were wars we'd go." He probed deeper, "Well, wouldn't that mean we could die?" Again, the depths of my 5 year olds questions were amazing to me. Was this God's way of confirming the call in my heart? I don't know, but my son was asking a very serious question, so I gave Him the only answer I knew to give. "Could we die?" I replied. "I guess so buddy. But, if God called us to a place where we could die, that must really mean there are people there who need to know Jesus. So we'd go. There are people right in Cheyenne who need to know Jesus too, so we're going there…because we're called."

That's really the reason I'm even writing this book. I'm not sure whom this book is meant to help. I don't know how many copies it will sell, how much of a difference it will make or if it's even any good. All I know is I'm writing it "Because I'm called". And so are you! God has placed a calling on your life. You may not even be aware of it yet, but it's there. Or perhaps you are aware of it, and it's burning in your heart but you don't know what to do, how you'll do it or what to expect. That's what I hope to help answer in this book.

My prayer is, as I share some of my story, the stories of people in my life and stories from the Bible; that what I've learned about being called will help other people discover their unique calling in life. So why should you keep reading? I guess you don't have to, but I would say, "Because you're called".

CHAPTER 1

What is a calling?

Everyone's called to SOMETHING but not everyone's called to the SAME thing!

If you're reading this book in the hopes that I'll tell you what *you're* called to do you'll be sorely disappointed. I could tell you to do some worthy, commendable, highly valuable things with your life, but they would never be fulfilling to you unless they are what *you're* called to do.

When it comes to your unique calling in life, only you and God are going to figure that one out. You might have some people in your life who you love and trust, love you in return and can help confirm your calling, but only you really know what it is *you're* called to do. I know, huge help, right?

I don't know what it is you're called to do. All I know is this: everyone's called to *something*. If you're a follower of Jesus, God has (or He will), place something in your heart that will make you say, "That's it! That's what I'm called to do." I'll get to that in a bit, but I need to back up first. The word "calling" by definition is this:

calling | ˈkôliNG |
noun
1) the loud cries or shouts of an animal or person: "the calling of a cuckoo." (If you're reading the book for that kind of calling you're wasting your time…just thought I'd throw that out there.)
2) [in sing.] a strong urge toward a particular way of life or career; a vocation: "those who have a special calling to minister to others' needs."
• a profession or occupation: he considered engineering one of the highest possible callings."

It's definition number two we typically think of as a "calling". Whatever career-field someone's in must be what *they* are called to do, but that's not necessarily the case. Many of you reading this book might be thinking, "If my career is my calling then it *sucks* to be called!" Hang in there and keep reading, because there is hope for you too.

A career and a calling could be two different things. Some people live out their calling *in* their career. I imagine that's where most of us want to be. I think it definitely makes it easier when your career *is* your calling. Other people have a career that funds their calling. Those people literally work a career they may not enjoy, to fund a calling that brings them joy. (If that's you, you inspire me! Keep it up!) Other people are in a career until they can live out their calling. They know what they're called to do; they just may not be able to do it yet for any number of reasons. Lastly, there are people who have a career but have *no* idea what they're called to do.

In every case, even the last one, all of us are called to something. One calling is not more significant than another. One calling is not more "right" than another. I've wrongly said before, "There is no greater calling than the calling to be a pastor." How stupid is that?

That's like telling everyone, "*My* calling is so much more important than *your* calling." What a horrible thing to say as a pastor. "Hey, I'm so much more important to God than you are. (insert evil laugh) I'm up here on the platform and God chose me to do the really important stuff while you just do the little, less important stuff down there. You wouldn't understand *my* calling because I have a *super* calling." It sounds about as dumb as wearing red underwear over blue tights looks.

For me to say there is no greater calling than to be a pastor means the woman called to be a stay at home mom is doing something less than me. It seriously makes me want to slap myself, which would be worth the price of the book for many of you! To all those who have ever heard me say that, I apologize. I mean that. Please forgive me. I was wrong…incredibly wrong.

The reality is this: everyone is called to *something*, but not everyone is called to the *same* thing. This can be incredibly liberating. You…yes *you*, are uniquely designed *by* God, to fulfill a God sized purpose *for* God. It may not be as a "pastor," in the career sense of the word. That's ok. In fact, it's great! If the world were full of nothing but pastors, who would work the other six days of the week? (That's a Pastor joke. Although some of you aren't laughing because you really do believe pastors work only one day each week.)

Ephesians 2:8-9 are some of the most oft quoted verses in the Bible. For many of you, I don't even need to print it in the book; it just rolls off your tongue. These two verses are the backbone of the Christian faith. They are what separate Christianity from every other religion on the planet. They say:

> **"God saved you by his grace when you believed. And you can't take credit for this; it is a *gift* from God. [9] Salvation is not a reward for the good things we have done, so none of us can boast about it." (NLT)**

And a collective "Amen!" resounds from the congregation, right? How great are those verses? We are saved by grace through faith! Literally, there is *nothing* we can do to be saved because *everything* has already been accomplished in our Savior. Any work toward our salvation would be empty, pointless and vain.

As I said, this separates Christianity from every other religion in the world. We cannot earn our salvation; no amount of money can buy it, there isn't enough hard work that can achieve it and we definitely do not deserve it, but it has been given to us through faith in Jesus. Wow! It's almost too much to bear.

Now, you might think, "Haven't we gotten off track here? Weren't we right in the middle of talking about our calling? I've already been converted, I want to know about my calling!" Yes, yes, patience my child. Maybe, that's what God's calling you to… patience. (If I were preaching, this is where I'd pause extra long in order to demonstrate patience, and the funny thing is, I actually paused my writing, but then I realized you're not at my desk, so the point would be lost in translation. So let me get on with my point.)

In the church, I hear these verses quoted all the time: "We're saved by grace through faith. We're saved by grace through faith. We're saved by grace through faith." And it's true, we are. But, if we fail to also quote verse ten, I think we are missing something very important, especially as it pertains to our calling.

Ephesians 2:10 *For* we are God's masterpiece. He has

created us anew in Christ Jesus, so we can *do* the good things he planned for us long ago (NLT).

What are those good things we're supposed to do? Could it be our calling? How do I know you are uniquely designed *by* God to fulfill a God-sized purpose *for* God? Because we're told so through the Apostle Paul. You are God's masterpiece! If you belong to Him, He has created you anew, and He has planned good things for you to do. I believe those good things are things God *has* called or *will* call only you to do.

I'm not saying you're the only person in the world who can be a pastor, or a stay at home mom, or a fireman or a (fill in the blank). I'm saying, as a pastor, as a stay at home mom, as a fireman, God has planned things that He's *only* planned for you to do; and you do them "because you're called".

God doesn't want you to be a pastor if you aren't called to be a pastor. He wants you to "do the good things He planned for you long ago." That's pretty amazing to me. How long was long ago? A year? Ten years? A hundred years? A million? The fact that God thought about *me*, and what He wanted to do *in* me and *through* me long ago, blows my mind. It puts some weight on my calling.

God doesn't just toss out some cool ideas for us to try. He takes a calling and places it on our lives. God thought about you before you were born and said, "What should I plan for him/her to do?" Then He planned it. If you know you're calling, this should make you more passionate about living it out than ever before. If you don't know you're calling, it should make you even more committed to discovering it. Let me say this again: God planned something for *you* to do long ago. Let that sink in.

So, when it comes to my unique calling in life, I could correctly say, "There is no greater calling on *my* life than that of being a pastor." And you can say the same thing too. So say it. What is it? Fill in the blank. Write it down. What is your calling? "There is no greater calling on my life than that of ________________!"

Did you write something? Is anything burning in your heart? If there isn't, it's okay! Maybe by the end of the book, there will be. But even if there's not, that's okay too. You're still called to something. You may not know your unique calling yet, but you still have a universal calling to live out. In fact, I believe it's in the universal calling of all followers of Jesus that we'll discover the unique calling on our lives. So let's go there…because you're called!

CHAPTER 2

Mr. Potato Head Christianity

Stop concerning yourself with God's will for your entire life, and start committing yourself to God's will for every day!

Ever since we've been married, I've told my wife that someone should start a restaurant called "I don't care!" That's a gold mine, right? I usually suggest this after asking my wife where she'd like to go out to eat, and her reply is "I don't care." Just once I'd love to say, "Ok" and drive her there for dinner.

There have even been occasions where she said, "I don't care," I'd make a suggestion, and she replied, "No…let's not go there!" "But you said you didn't care!" There have been times I've sat in the driveway for several minutes trying to discover where my wife wanted to go out to eat. And if she's pregnant, forget it! (This is more of an indictment on me not planning a date well than it is on her being indecisive.) Ever been stuck in that scenario with someone before? If you have, then you've experienced the exact frustration I'm describing. (I'm telling you, a restaurant with that name would be *huge*! Perhaps that's someone's calling.)

Multiply by one thousand the frustration level of trying to figure out where someone wants to go out to eat, and I think we would be close to how frustrated many of us feel about the will of God. I believe so many people are just sitting in the driveway of life, waiting for God to reveal to them what He wants them to do.

One of the most common questions I hear from people about life is, "How do I know God's will?" Or more specifically, "What is God's will for my life? What have I been put on earth to do?"

Those are great questions, but I wonder if we haven't made them more difficult than they need to be. I wonder if we haven't made "finding God's will" into a giant game of hide and seek. As if we go off and count while God hides His will somewhere, and then we're required to keep on looking for it until we somehow happen to find it.

Here's something we all need to understand; God's ultimate desire is that you *know* His will because His highest purpose for your life is that you *live* in His will. God wants you to know His will for your life more than *you* want to know His will for your life. That's very encouraging!

The bad news is, there aren't very many times in the Bible where it says, "God's will is," and then makes a blanket statement that applies to us all. I did a quick word search on a Bible website for the phrase "God's will" across all translations. Here's what I found.

The words "God's will" are used together thirty-two times in the Bible. Four of those verses specifically apply to everyone. I then found two other verses that refer to what God "wants" for everyone. Six total verses about God's will as something specific, that anyone could read and apply to themself. For those who are wondering, here they are:

Be thankful in all circumstances, for this is *God's will* for you who belong to Christ Jesus.
(1 Thessalonians 5:18 NLT)

***God's will* is for you to be holy…**
(1 Thessalonians 4:3 NLT)

It is *God's will* that your honorable lives should silence those ignorant people who make foolish accusations against you. (1 Peter 2:15 NLT)

For *God's will* was for us to be made holy by the sacrifice of the body of Jesus Christ, once for all time. (Hebrews 10:10 NLT)

(Speaking of God) **…*who wants* everyone to be saved and to understand the truth.**
(1 Timothy 2:4 NLT)

***He does not want* anyone to be destroyed, but *wants everyone* to repent. (2 Peter 3:9 NLT)**

I'm fully aware that there are other, clear indications in the Bible about what God wants that I did not include here. The ten commandments are kind of a biggie. Loving each other, forgiveness and faith stand out. Not cheering for the Denver Broncos and never owning a cat! (Can I get an amen?) Those are just a few. The six verses mentioned above though are the ones I've found that clearly state, "This is God's will."

Call me simple, but I truly believe that Christianity is a series of next steps. We're not always going to see down the road. We won't always see around the corner, but I am confident we *can* know what our next step is. The most important step any of us can ever take in life is leaping off the pages of this book through those verses we just read. BELIEVE – IN – JESUS!

It is "God's will" that everyone repent and be saved through faith in Christ, and then live in the holiness that *only* He can provide. God *wants* us…He's *chosen* us…it's His *will* for us…He's *called* us to be in relationship with Him. It's the greatest piece of God's will you'll ever know. What does that mean for you?

It means today, if you're not in relationship with God through His Son Jesus, then the only step you need to take is surrendering your heart to Him. God's *only* will for your life right now is to forgive you of your sins, come into your heart, make you new and start a relationship with you. Nothing else in your life right now matters as much to God than that. In fact, God wants you to be in relationship with Him so much; He gave His only son Jesus to accomplish that.

John 3:16 says, **"For God so loved the world that he gave his one and only Son, that whoever believes in him shall not perish but have eternal life" (NIV).**

Perhaps you're reading this right now and you've never nailed down the issue of your eternity. You've never experienced the forgiveness of your sins through turning to Jesus and putting your faith in Him for salvation. If that's you and you're ready to take that next step in your life but don't know what to do, don't know what to say, or don't know what it means, you can turn to page number 98 and find something written specifically for you there. Go ahead and go…I'll wait for you right here.

Once you've nailed down the issue of your eternity, you've got to nail down the issue of every day. "How do I know God's will for my life?" "What have I been put on earth to do?" Well, if Christianity is a series of next steps with salvation being the first, then whether you've been a Christian for fifty years, fifty months, fifty weeks, fifty days or fifty seconds, He has a next step for you. The great news is He wants you to know what that step is.

In **Romans 12:2** The Apostle Paul says this, **"*Then* you will learn to know God's will for you, which is good and pleasing and perfect" (NLT).** This tells us it's possible to know God's will *and* there is something we can do to know it.

Knowing God's will is actually an amazing concept to think about. In **Isaiah 55:9** God says, **"For just as the heavens are higher than the earth, so my ways are higher than your ways and my thoughts higher than your thoughts" (NLT).** And Paul says, "*Then* you will learn to know God's will." Or in other words, "*Then* you will learn to know the mind of God," or at least the parts that pertain to your life. So when is *then*?

When it comes to God's will, I think we often expect pastors and teachers to offer some deep, confusing, theological response. We tend to believe that finding God's will is going to be difficult. It must be a high and lofty ordeal using some complicated formula. Surely God's will is hard to come by. After all, He's *God*! That's just not the case.

Remember, God's ultimate desire is that you *know* His will because His highest purpose for your life is that you *live* in His will. So if His highest purpose for your life is that you live in His will, don't you think He wants you to know what it is? "*Then* you will learn to know God's will for you…" When is then? Let's go back one verse in Romans 12, to verse number one.

> **And so, dear brothers and sisters, I plead with you to *give your bodies to God* because of all he has done for you. Let them be a living and holy sacrifice—the kind he will find acceptable. This is**

> **truly the way to worship him. *Then* you will learn to know God's will for you...**
>
> **(Romans 12:1-2a NLT)**

In order to know God's will, we must give Him our bodies. Let me say this as clearly as I can: God wants your body! I know that sounds weird and maybe even a little awkward to say, but it's true! This is part of the universal calling of all followers of Jesus.

"God wants your body," means exactly what it says in those verses. We must offer up our bodies as a living sacrifice --- the kind He will find acceptable. And if you think about it, it really is the only appropriate response to all God has done for us.

The original readers of the book of Romans would have been early Jewish Christians. So when they heard the term "living sacrifice," they likely would have drawn a correlation to the Old Testament sacrificial system found in Leviticus. They would have known that the only acceptable sacrifice to God was an animal slain on the altar then used up and/or burned up completely.

> **Then the priest will burn the *entire* sacrifice on the altar as a burnt offering. It is a special gift, a pleasing aroma to the LORD.**
>
> **(Leviticus 1:9b NLT)**

Every day in the temple this would occur. A sacrifice would be offered to God on the altar, and then it would be used up and/or burned up completely. The legs, eyes, head, interior, *all* of it would be completely given to God for His purpose and for His glory. That was the picture these readers would have had in mind. So, what does this mean for us?

Well, as opposed to the dead sacrifices offered up every day in the temple, we are to offer our bodies as a *living* sacrifice. We are to give God our bodies...*all* of it. God wants your body!

I love the language Paul uses here. He really leaves no doubt. If he were to ask us, "Do I make myself clear?" We would have to respond like Tom Cruise in, *A Few Good Men* with, "Crystal!" Our response to all God has done for us, and the *when* before the *then* in knowing His will, is to give Him our bodies. Nothing in and of ourselves can escape being surrendered to God. Nothing! Our head, our mind, our eyes, our mouth, our ears, our feet, our hands, *everything* must be given to God. It *all* belongs to Him, and it *all* should be used for Him.

So in order to know God's will, I have to give God my body? Yes, but there is one problem. We often live in a state of what I like to call "Mr. Potato Head Christianity".

Imagine yourself right now as a giant Mr. or Mrs. Potato Head. Often times, we come to God saying something like, "God, I give you my life," which is not as specific as "I give you my body." It lets us off the hook a bit. "My life is yours, God!" But not really, because we keep our hands over here and our eyes over there and our mouth...well, we're not ready to surrender our mouth yet. Isn't that how we often live?

We love Mr. Potato Head Christianity. In that kind of life, we can keep our community eyes separate from our church eyes, our work mouth separate from our worship mouth, and our private mind separate from our public mind. We can use our body parts according to the setting we are in, and more for our pleasure than for God's purpose.

However, if Paul was making a direct reference to the Old Testament sacrificial system, then if an animal that was sacrificed without its entire body was not accepted by God, why would we think God will accept our sacrifice, or reveal any more of His will to us if we're not willing to surrender all of our bodies to Him?

"What's God's will for my life?" Here is something I'm learning to understand. God's not going to show us His will for our entire life if we're not willing to live in His will for every day. God's will for every day is that we give Him our bodies! *All* of it! Used up and/or burned up completely on His altar. Fully used for Him and His glory!

We don't get to pick and choose what parts of God's will we get to do. The parts of His will we already know are the parts of His will we should already be doing. What a lot of us must decide is to simply *do* what we already *know*. Many times we want God to reveal something new in our lives because we don't want to live in what we already know. We ask, "How can I get God's will to match my desire?" Because when God's will matches our desire we have no problem living in it, right?

What we should be saying is, "How can I get my desire to match God's will?" We can only make our desire match God's will by giving God our bodies. You want to know what God's will is? Place your body on the altar, and I guarantee you, something will rise to the top.

Now, you're not going to say, "Okay God, I'm all yours," climb on the altar and everything is fixed in your life. His will for your life won't be displayed in neon lights and His plan for your future won't be written on paper and delivered to your door. You might say, "Ok God, I'm all yours," climb on the altar and He's going to start pointing out areas of your life that need to come under His control. (Back to Mr. Potato Head) "Hey, Jeff, those hands over there; let me have those." And you'll surrender them to God. "Ok God, now I'm *all* yours." "Hey, Jeff, those ears over there, let me have those."

He'll ask for relationships, habits, attitudes and priorities. When you give God your body, you'll never lack knowing His will. There will *always* be something else to do or somewhere else to go. He'll want to mold something in your life, adjust something in your heart or be Lord over an area you've yet to surrender. This is all part of God's sanctifying process as you allow Him to change you more and more into the image of His Son! Getting on the altar may happen in a single step, but staying on the altar requires a continual surrender. It's an every day thing. The every day will of God!

This is where I think we've made knowing God's will too difficult. Stop concerning yourself with God's will for your *entire life* and start committing yourself to God's will for *every day.* Because guess what? If you live out God's will for every day and then do it again tomorrow, extrapolate that out and you'll end up accomplishing His will for your entire life.

Paul goes on to say, **"Don't copy the behavior and customs of this world, but let God transform you by *changing the way you think.*" (Romans 12:2a)**

This is so crucial. If we give God our bodies but don't change the way we think, we'll never understand God's will. How do we change the way we think? You change the way you think by getting God's Word into your heart. You cannot know the will of God apart from being in the Word of God. It's amazing to me how many Christians say they want to know God's will, but refuse to regularly pick up and read His Word.

I believe God's Word reveals His will for every area of our lives. The more you get God's Word in your heart, the more you'll think about God's Word. The more you think about God's Word, the more you'll know His will. The more you know God's will, the more you'll live in your calling. So give God your body. Change the way you think, and *then* you will learn to know God's will for you. It's a process, and it's in this process you'll end up finding your calling.

Climb on the altar…because you're called!

CHAPTER 3

Jesus' Bride, not my backup plan

The Church is Jesus' bride, not a backup plan when the weekend vacation falls through.

When it comes to our universal calling, we're all called to three things. We've covered the first two already:

1.) We're called to Christ through salvation.
2.) We're called to change through sanctification (Giving God our body)

The third is we are called to God's Church through our serving.

There is a calling for every follower of Jesus staring us straight in the face we often ignore. We're so consumed with our career, our "calling" or our comfort that we miss the one thing Jesus said *He* would build. The Church! "*I* will build the church," Jesus said. How does He propose to build it? With you and I!

Each of us, as followers of Jesus, has been given a spiritual gift. Call them abilities, talents, passions or whatever you want, but *God* is the one who gives them, and *we* are responsible to use them to build His Church.

> **A spiritual *gift* is given to each of us so we can help *each other.* (The Church)**
>
> **(1 Corinthians 12:7 NLT)**
>
> **God has given each of you a *gift* from his great variety of spiritual gifts. Use them well to *serve one another.* (The Church) (1 Peter 4:10 NLT)**
>
> **In his grace, God has given us different gifts for doing certain things well. So if God has given you the ability to prophesy, speak out with as much faith as God has given you. If your gift is serving others, serve them well. If you are a teacher, teach well. If your gift is to encourage others, be encouraging. If it is giving, give generously. If God has given you leadership ability, take the responsibility seriously. And if you have a gift for showing kindness to others, do it gladly.**
>
> **(Romans 12:6-8 NLT)**

Yes, you can and should use your gifts in the unique calling God gives you, but the reason I'm writing about this in this book is because I believe the best place to find your unique calling in God's Kingdom is to live out the universal calling to serve His Church. How can I live out a calling on my *life* if I'm not first committed to the calling of my *Lord*..."*I* will build my Church?"

If you're a follower of Jesus and not currently plugged into a church, *that* is your next step. If you are in a church but not currently serving it's mission and vision with your gifts and talents through volunteering, then *that* is your next step. The church is Jesus' bride, not a backup plan when the weekend vacation falls through.

You want to know what your calling is? Start serving in the church. Regardless of how long it takes...whether God reveals

His calling for your life in a week or in 20 years, the calling to serve His Church never goes away…*ever*! Why do I press in on this so heavily? Because I've seen first hand how God has re-directed people's careers because He called them while serving in His Church.

I have an obvious bent towards ministry. I view calling through the lens of being a pastor. It's really all I've ever known. My Great Grandfather was a pastor, my Grandfather was a pastor, my Dad is a pastor and now I'm serving in full time ministry as a pastor. My experience and knowledge on calling are guided from that perspective, so the best first hand experiences I have with calling are that of full time ministry.

I know a calling goes much farther than ministry. We established in chapter one that one calling is not better or more "right" than another. The only "right" calling for you is the one God's given you. There are countless stories, both present and past, of people discovering and living out their calling outside of full time ministry.

You're probably already thinking of some people who have inspired you through their stories. One person who immediately comes to my mind is Blake Mycoskie, who through TOMS, the company he started in 2006, has given away over two million pairs of shoes to children in need.

TOMS began while Blake was traveling in Argentina and saw many children growing up without shoes. The solution? A calling to start a business where one purchase of shoes for you would in turn, send a pair to a child in need. It was revolutionary to say the least. TOMS just expanded its vision to a One for One eyewear line. (www.toms.com)

Jessica Jackley and Matt Flannery started an organization called Kiva in 2003. Their calling was inspired while listening to a lecture at Stanford Business School. Kiva allows people to lend money through the Internet to entrepreneurs in developing countries who otherwise couldn't afford to start their business, school, organization, etc. Through May 2013, Kiva has distributed $437,054,600 in loans from 938,049 lenders to 1,050,587 borrowers. (www.kiva.org)

At the age of 18 with a desire to make a difference, Katie Davis headed out for a missions trip to Uganda over her Christmas break, and in the process, her life was flipped upside down. While on the trip, Katie was so moved by the needs of the people that she knew her calling was to come back and be a part of caring for their needs. The result was a complete change in the direction of her life. Katie moved to Uganda where she now lives out her calling, and currently has adopted 14 Ugandan children who had been orphaned.
(http://kissesfromkatie.blogspot.com/ and http://www.amazima.org/katiesbook.html)

Here are the stories two of current full-time staff members at Element Church who found their *unique* calling in life because they were living in the *universal* calling of all followers of Jesus. I hope their stories will inspire you in your calling.

Derek Mowery – Full-time Children's Pastor at Element Church since September of 2009.

Derek accepted Christ at the age of 10 while attending a small Baptist church in Greybull, WY. He quickly grew in his faith, but fell away from God when his newfound freedom after high school graduation set in. Derek said, "Sometimes it's hard to believe how easily I walked away from God once I was on my own."

After years of destructive living, Derek realized his choices were not only affecting himself, but also his wife and children. In 2006, he experienced a spiritual rock bottom that caused him to turn his life back over to God again. "My life felt empty and hopeless despite how it looked from the outside, and I cried out for God to take me back."

After recommitting his life to Christ, he began to seek God in every decision of his life. He started attending church again with his family, spending time in the Bible, serving other people and leading his family in a godly way. In 2007, Derek began to pray a "dangerous prayer." He started asking God to use him somewhere. "It doesn't matter where," Derek would pray, "Just use me!" That's exactly what God did.

God began to answer Derek's dangerous prayer through His Church. Derek would pray, "Should I be doing more in the church?" God then used a weekend message to get him serving in the kid's ministry as a leader.

He would pray, "Should I be working less at my job and giving more time to the church?" and God answered with a better paying position at work which allowed more free time in his schedule.

He would pray, "A church would be crazy to let me lead, but I think I could make a difference if they did. If this feeling is real, God, *You're* going to have to make it happen." God answered this prayer by using a staff member to say, "Have you ever thought about full-time ministry?"

Within several months of that comment, God had Derek sitting in front of the Leadership Team of Element Church talking about serving as the volunteer kid's ministry director. As the church grew, so did the responsibility of his position, so he started praying, "God I need some relief from my job so I can dig into this church thing." The church then offered him a full time job.

"It all started," Derek says "by repenting from my selfish living. That turned into a commitment to serve God wherever He needed me, which turned into a unique calling on my life. My calling was confirmed in my heart by the Holy Spirit and then confirmed through the men leading God's church who were asking God for the same thing I was offering Him…*me*!"

(Derek currently leads the kid's ministry at Element Church with over 300 children learning about Jesus every week)

Steve Doolin – Full-time Outreach Director and Volunteer Coordinator at Element Church since January of 2012.

Steve was born a preacher's kid and the youngest of three children. He was raised in the church his entire life and says, "The Christian faith was really forced upon me, even when I didn't understand it or had hard questions." Eventually, following Jesus was the furthest thing from his mind, and he began to live for his own purpose instead of the purpose of Christ.

While living in Tacoma, Washington, Steve became involved in a tagging crew (graffiti) and in his words, "other things unbecoming of a preacher's kid." At the age of 16, his family relocated to Sheridan, Wyoming, where he easily found trouble once again, which pulled him even farther away from Jesus. He walked in and out of relationship with God throughout his teens and twenties, never really understanding or pursuing Him.

At the age of 31, Steve was divorced with two boys of his own to help raise. He was living a desperate, lonely life and disliked most people he came across, including himself. A young lady named Chaney came into Steve's life. As they spent more time together she began to challenge him with her desire for a marriage where

Jesus was at the center and the spiritual leader of the home was her husband. "This was a foreign concept to me," Steve said. "Quite frankly it made me mad."

After wrestling with that challenge from Chaney for a while, God began to reveal to Steve that this was *His* desire for marriage as well, which eventually led to their wedding in June of 2007. It didn't take long for Steve to see that living inside of God's plan for marriage, and for life, opens up the window to God's blessing.

They began looking as a family for a church they could call "home." Chaney had heard about a new church meeting in a theater and suggested they try it. With some hesitation to the idea of a church at the movies, they checked out Element Church and immediately fell in love. Steve began to get plugged in to serving by drawing and painting set designs, but he still wasn't sold on serving regularly in the church until the head usher at Element challenged him to serve on his team.

It started as helping as an usher on a bi-weekly basis and Steve soon found great joy in helping other people find life; which was something very new to him. He continued ushering for some time, then became a greeter, and then was asked to run a project in the church's outreach ministry. The project entailed mobilizing and organizing teams to remodel a duplex home which Element had purchased, to provide short-term affordable housing to people who were in need, specifically single moms.

During his work on the house, God began stirring Steve's heart for more ministry opportunities. Shortly after completing the housing project, he approached the leaders of Element and shared the calling God had placed on his life. Steve said, "My leaders were receptive to my desire, yet they encouraged me to figure out what my calling looked like specifically and to pray about the right timing of it."

He continued to volunteer in many capacities in the church and eventually was offered a part-time position as the church's Outreach Coordinator. For nearly a year and a half, Steve continued working his fulltime job for the State of Wyoming, while also working part time for Element Church; all the while God was expanding the calling that was placed within him. Eventually, in January of 2012, Steve embarked on his journey into full-time ministry at Element.

Currently, Steve is the Outreach and Volunteer Coordinator leading hundreds of volunteers and numerous outreach projects. He said, "I *love* my job! I never would have dreamed I would be in a position where I deal with hundreds of people from week to week, yet God has placed me here! He continues to stir my heart and mold the ministry in which I lead. I am humbled and blessed at the role the 'local church' has played in my calling."

While not everyone who volunteers *in* the church will eventually be called into full-time ministry *for* the church, I firmly believe that without Derek and Steve's commitment to God's Church, they never would have experienced His calling in the Kingdom. It's in living out the universal calling to serve the Church that I believe you'll best discover your unique calling in God's Kingdom.

So where are you? Have you given your life to Christ? Have you given God your body? Are you committed to God's Church? If so, buckle up, because the ride has just begun. As you live out your universal calling as a follower of Jesus, God will begin to open doors, provide opportunities, and create divine appointments for a unique calling on your life like you would never dream...because you're called.

CHAPTER 4

Faith and Foreskin

God won't ask you to do something significant for Him until you're willing to do what you consider small.

We hear the word "calling" and we immediately think "colossal". In fact, I believe calling and colossal go hand in hand in our minds. Everyone wants to do something significant. *Everyone*! No one talks about stories of simplicity; they're always stories of significance.

If you're a pastor, you want to lead a large church, with amazing stories of God's provision and life change, or preach to an audience of thousands like Billy Graham, Rick Warren or Andy Stanley. If you're a businessperson, you want to run a business that's innovative and market changing like Apple, Google or Facebook. If you're an athlete, you want to hit the walk-off home run, score the game-winning touchdown or hit the buzzer-beating shot.

We want to discover cures for diseases, rescue the damsel in distress, and start companies like Toms or Kiva, which bring hope into the world. In Sunday School, what stories made the flannel graph board? It definitely wasn't the steady Eddy that just kept following God every day. (I either completely lost you with the flannel graph comment, or took some of you right back in time to a musty, cinder block basement of an old church building somewhere with a Sunday School teacher who smelled like Ben Gay. And you'll also be singing Father Abraham for the rest of the day! You're welcome!)

The stories we learned growing up in church were the colossal ones. Noah building a giant boat to ride out the storm. David slaying Goliath. Moses raising his staff to part the Red Sea. Esther taking a stand for God's people against their adversary. Shadrach, Meshach and Abednego boldly standing among the flames of the furnace in defiance of the King. Daniel surviving the lion's den unscathed. Peter preaching one sermon and three thousand people being saved and baptized. Paul raising people from the dead. Those are just a few of the big stories.

One mention of those stories gets us fired up. We hear stories like that and we're ready to charge the gates of hell with a water pistol. We love the colossal, don't we? We all want to change the world. We not only want to *do* something significant, but we want to *be* someone significant.

I don't remember a flannel graph story about John the Baptist getting his head cut off. There were no stories of "the others" from Hebrews chapter 11. We call that chapter the "Hall of Faith" in the Church, but we kind of taper off our enthusiasm towards the end because it talks about those who were tortured, persecuted, chained in prison, sawed in two, stoned and killed with the sword.

Now that I think about it, that wouldn't be very good Sunday School material, would it? Little Johnny had a hard enough time being dropped off in Sunday School, and the last thing his parents need are nightmares about someone being sawed in two and people's heads falling off. My point remains the same though: Even as adults, we love the stories of significance.

If you're like me, you read the Bible stories as if *you're* the main character. *You* are the hero. No one ever reads about David and Goliath and says, "I think I'm gonna play the role of Goliath today! I just feel like being slain." No one wants to be King Nebuchadnezzar, throwing three teenage boys into a flaming furnace. No one's ever a disciple in the boat while Peter walks on water. We're never a pea on top of the walls of Jericho taunting Joshua and his army before it falls. (Sorry, I'm a parent of young children. I often read the Bible through *Veggie Tale* eyes.)

We're always the heroes of the story, right? Part of the reason we're always the heroes is, not only do we love the colossal, but we also tend to read the Bible and Christian history, with hindsight. As they say, hindsight is 20/20. We know the rest of the story, so we subconsciously interject that the participants must have too, which makes what they accomplished much easier.

What we often fail to recognize with the Bible heroes we grew up learning about, and quite frankly still idolize today, is they didn't know the rest of the story. They didn't know what God was *going* to do; they were just doing the next thing He *told* them to do. Input Joshua!

I say, "Joshua," and what do you immediately think of? Jericho! Leader! Warrior! Prayed for the sun to stand still, and it did! "As for me and my house, we will serve the Lord!" Book of the Bible. Seriously, if you have a book of the Bible named after you, that's pretty cool!

When we hear "Joshua," we typically think of everything starting in chapter 6 of the book named after him. Outside of God saying,

"I will never leave you or forsake you" in chapter 1, we really don't know much about Joshua before chapter 6. But without Joshua chapters 1 – 5, there *are* no Joshua chapters 6-24.

I love the story of Joshua. Every time I read through that book, it seems like I see something new, am reminded of something I forgot or am challenged, convicted or comforted in some way. There is one principle though that defines the book of Joshua for me, and I believe it defines the calling on our lives as followers of Christ. From Joshua chapter 1, all the way through the end of the book; crisis after crisis, event after event, battle after battle, victory after victory this principle is always there:

God won't ask you to do something *significant* for Him unless you're willing to do what you consider *small.*

I think the theme chapter of Joshua is not chapter 6 and the conquering of Jericho. Call me a heretic, but it's not even Joshua chapter 1 with God promising His presence and provision. The theme chapter of Joshua is chapter 5. To be specific, the theme passage is chapter 5 verses 2-3. Allow me to set the stage.

In Joshua chapter 1, Moses has died and God appoints Joshua as the new leader of Israel. God says to Joshua in chapter 1 verse 2, **"Moses my servant is dead."** I always laugh when I read that. God just got to the point didn't he? It's almost as if Joshua is frozen in fear and God's trying to slap him out of it.

Maybe Joshua thought Moses would come back, or that he wasn't really dead in the first place. He had gone away on a mountain on more than one occasion before and come back. Maybe he'll come back this time.

"Moses my servant is dead." I think God was saying to Joshua, "You're it, bro! He ain't coming back. I buried him myself.

(Deuteronomy 34:6 reference) So it's time for you to lead these people." And then we read the famous promise of God's presence and provision in Joshua's life: **"I will never leave you nor forsake you." (NIV)**

In Joshua chapter 2, the spies are sent out into Jericho to scout out the city.

In Joshua chapter 3, the Israelites cross the Jordan River on dry ground.

In Joshua chapter 4, they set up a memorial altar of praise to God for parting the Jordan.

Then we hit Joshua chapter 5, the theme passage of the entire book. **Joshua 5:2-3** says this: **At that time the LORD told Joshua, "Make flint knives and *circumcise* this second generation of Israelites."** [3] **So Joshua made flint knives and circumcised the entire male population of Israel at Gibeath-haaraloth. (NLT)**

Man, props to Joshua! I must say, I might have quit right there. I'm struck sometimes, convicted really, at the rapid obedience of people in the Bible. There are so many examples of God speaking a word to His children, and they just simply do it, and I don't know if there is any better example of that in the Bible than Joshua.

Read Joshua chapters 1 – 5 sometime and notice how many times it says, "The Lord told Joshua to…So Joshua did."

(Joshua 1:2 & 1:10-11) **The Lord told Joshua** that the time had come to lead the Israelites across the Jordan River. **So Joshua commanded** the leaders of Israel to gather the people and let them know in three days we will cross the Jordan.

(Joshua 3:7-13) **The Lord told Joshua** that when you get to the edge of the Jordan, command the priests to take a few steps into the river. (Which was in flood stage by the way, and the water was overflowing its banks) **So Joshua told the people** that the priests would step in the water, and when they did, the flow of water would stop.

(Joshua 4:1-9) **The Lord told Joshua** to choose twelve men who would take twelve stones out of the riverbed and make a memorial of God's provision. **So Joshua called the men** he had selected and told them to set up a memorial.

(Joshua 4:15-17) **The Lord told Joshua** to command the priests to come out of the water. **So Joshua told** the priests to come up out of the water.

The very next time the Lord told Joshua to do something was Joshua chapter 5. ... **"the LORD told Joshua, 'Make flint knives and *circumcise* this second generation of Israelites.'"**

Put yourself in Joshua's shoes. Seriously! We read past these verses as if, "Oh yeah, circumcision, no big deal." REALLY? Imagine walking into a meeting at your church, business, organization or family and saying, "Alright guys. Today, I'm going to circumcise you because *God* told me to." You thought your meetings were tense already.

If I were Joshua, my response may have been quite different. "Pardon me God, but did you say *circumcise*? Maybe your Hebrew is not as good as mine. I mean, I know you invented the language and all, but I think you got your words mixed up. Did you mean *circle* the wagons? I can do that no problem. Or maybe perform a *circus*? That's tougher, but I'll figure it out. But *circumcise*? That thing they do to baby boys, and they scream like they're about to die? That kind of circumcise?"

I'd have been dancing around the issue for quite some time, but not Joshua. The Lord told Joshua to… **"So Joshua made flint knives and circumcised the entire male population of Israel at Gibeath-haaraloth."**

Two leadership thoughts here:

1.) The greatest testament to Joshua's leadership may not have been his *willingness* to circumcise the men, but the fact that those men were willing to *let* him. There must have been a level of trust in Joshua that few leaders ever see.
2.) If you quit just because you're *uncomfortable*, you'll never see God do the *unthinkable*.

Do you know what the very next thing God accomplished through Joshua was *after* the circumcision? Conquering Jericho. You might say, "Well, if God asked me to do something significant like that, I'd say yes too." We need to understand in our calling that God will never ask you to do something *significant* for Him until you're willing to do something you consider *small.*

The Lord told Joshua to…so Joshua did. That was the story of his calling. The power to conquer Jericho simply came from a pattern of obedience in his life. The biggest test and the biggest task in Joshua's life was not Jericho. We've made it out to be, but it's not. The biggest test and the biggest task in Joshua's life was the one before it: circumcision.

Joshua didn't know that Jericho would be the next thing; He was just doing the next thing God asked him to do. If Joshua had not been willing to take the step of circumcision, He never would have seen the significance of Jericho. God knew that Joshua had the faith to conquer Jericho because Joshua had the foreskins to prove it.

The most significant thing you'll ever do in your life is simply the very next thing God's asking you to do; and if you don't take that small step, you may never be asked to take the significant one either. Yet that's exactly where so many people live their lives, somewhere between what was and what could be. Somewhere between faith and foreskins. So take that next step, even if it's small. No, *especially* if it's small…because you're called!

CHAPTER 5

How do I *know* I'm called?

If you can do anything else and not be in sin you're not called! – Pastor Dan Morgan

I'll never forget hearing that phrase for the first time. I don't know if it's original to Pastor Dan, but he's the only person I've ever heard it from and I think it's the best definition of being called.

Dan Morgan is the Senior Pastor of the church I led youth ministry in while living in Gillette, Wyoming. At the time we had a staff member who was struggling with their place in ministry, specifically full-time ministry. They thought it's what they were supposed to do, but they didn't know for sure.

Sitting in this young man's office, I listened as he explained the difficulty he was facing of knowing, "Am I called to this position or not?" I don't remember if these were his exact words, but in some form or fashion he asked Pastor Dan and I, "How do you know you're called?"

Before this conversation took place, I'd always felt like explaining a "call" was like explaining how you know when you're in love, or how you know whom you're supposed to marry. "You just know!" had always been my answer. It's a cop-out answer if you think about it. We tend to give answers like that when we don't know the answer or don't want to tell the answer. Like when your kid asks you where babies come from. "Ask your mom," is always a good one, or "God makes babies." That last one seemed to always work until my 5-year-old daughter asked me, "Well, *how* does God make the babies?" My response was not so smart. "He uses mommy's and daddy's." Can you guess what the next question was? "Well, *how* does God use mommy's and daddy's?" "Ummmm, ask your mom!" But I digress.

"How do you know you're called?" was this young man's question, and I'll never forget what Pastor Dan said. It has forever changed the way I view a calling. He said this: "If you can do anything else besides this (specific ministry) and not be in sin, you're *not* called." Wow!

When it comes to our unique calling in life, it cannot be just a good idea, or a strong desire. It's not something you think would be fun, or fulfilling, although when you live in your calling it should be both of those things. A calling, as I see it, is something you cannot shake, you won't be talked out of and you can't be persuaded otherwise. It's none other than a mandate from God.

The prophet Jeremiah put it this way: **"But if I say I'll never mention the LORD or speak in his name, his word burns in my heart like a fire. It's like a fire in my bones! I am worn out trying to hold it in! I can't do it!" (Jeremiah 20:19 NLT)** Jeremiah was clear. "Whether I want to or not, I am compelled to do this. I cannot stop, and I cannot hold it in. This is my calling."

The Apostle Paul said something similar as recorded in the book of **Acts 20:22-24**. He wrote: **"And now, *compelled* by the Spirit, I am going to Jerusalem, not knowing what will**

happen to me there. I only know that in every city the Holy Spirit warns me that prison and hardships are facing me. However, I consider my life worth nothing to me; my *only* aim is to finish the race and *complete the task the Lord Jesus has given me*—the task of testifying to the good news of God's grace.

Paul's ultimate desire was to finish the task…the *calling* God had placed upon his life. What was his calling? "Testifying to the good news of God's grace." If you read the continuing account in the book of Acts, you'll even find well-meaning people who tried to talk Paul out of his calling. They tried to convince him not to go to Jerusalem because they too knew that "suffering" was ahead. Paul would have none of it. He was compelled…bound…*called* by God. When you're called by God, you cannot be convinced otherwise.

It reminds me of one of the scenes from my all time favorite movie, *Hoosiers*. In the film, Coach Norman Dale (played by Gene Hackman) was leading a rag tag group of young men on the Hickory Husker high school basketball team. Before the movie is halfway over, the entire town had turned against Coach Dale, including some of his players and closest friends, due to the team's poor performance.

Through a series of climactic events, most notably the star player (Jimmy Chitwood) rejoining the team in the middle of a town hall meeting meant to fire Coach Dale, the team begins to turn their season around, and the players were united behind the vision of Coach Dale. At one point, when challenging an assistant coach to step up and stand out he said: "I didn't think I could cut it the other night, either, but after what Jimmy did, it would take the Indiana National Guard to get me out of here."

I describe my calling that way as well. It would take the Wyoming National Guard to remove me from leading Element Church and being in full-time ministry. Doing what I do is like a "fire in my bones." I am compelled…bound…*called* to do what I do. For me, it would be a sin to do anything else because *this* is what God has called me to do. How did I *kbow* I was called?

Well, I don't know how it's worked for you or will work for you, but God has *always* used His Word to confirm my call. That's why I can assuredly say what I already said before, "You cannot know the *will* of God outside of being in the *Word* of God."

I once heard a pastor wisely say, "I can't prove to you that God exists. I can only bring you to a place where the two of you might meet." In the same way, I can't prove to you that you're called; I can only share with you how God has called *me* and pray that He awakens or confirms something in *you*…because you're called.

CHAPTER 6

Will the real Jeff Maness please stand up?

Many are the plans in a man's heart,
but it is the Lord's purpose that prevails.
– Proverbs 19:21

I have a twin brother named Jeremy. For a lot of you it can be really scary to know there is someone else out there like me. I can honestly say that throughout my life, he has been my closest friend, and remains so to this day. We did everything together growing up. *Everything*! So much so that when we headed off to college, we were going to get our degrees in business and accounting and then open our own business together. (Why I ever wanted to be in accounting I'll never know.)

We headed off to college with dreams of eventually owning and operating our own sporting goods store. If I remember correctly, we even talked about having a ministry aspect to it where we could have a gym/recreation area that would be opened up to kids who were less fortunate.

Our plan was in place. Not only were we classmates, but we were roommates. As far I was concerned, we'd be that way all through college and at least in close partnership beyond that. *Great* plan…but God had a different purpose.

During Christmas break of our Sophomore year of college, I attended a Christian youth conference in Cincinnati, OH, with our church youth group. My brother and his fiancé were there as well, along with my future brother-in-law, who was in high school at the time and already surrendered his life to a calling in full-time ministry.

I could take you to the exact spot in that giant auditorium of the downtown Cincinnati convention center where God poked my heart with a fire I would not be able to contain, even though I tried. I can't tell you who was speaking that night. I can't tell you what he spoke on or anything else from that day. But my view of the platform, and what happened at the end of that service, will forever be etched in my mind.

The speaker began talking about being "called into full-time ministry." Immediately, something began stirring in my heart. Something was tugging, pulling, drawing, and compelling me. Whether I was paying attention before that moment I don't know, but at this point I was hanging on every word.

He talked about Moses from the Old Testament and the story where Aaron and Hur had to hold up his hands during a battle against the Amalekites. (Exodus 17) As long as Moses' hands, while holding the staff were raised in the air, the Israelites would be victorious. The speaker equated this to full-time ministry and said that those who were "called" needed people around them to "hold up their hands." He then said to this group of a few thousand young people, "If you are here this evening and God has called you into full time ministry, I want you to stand up right where you are."

In that moment, everything within me was trying to stand while everything outside me made sure I stayed in my seat. I knew, right then, God was calling me into the ministry, but I didn't *want* to go in the ministry. I wanted to start a business with my best friend. As I said, my dad, granddad and great granddad were all pastors, and I was *not* going to be a pastor.

Sitting right next to me was my future brother-in-law. I had been dating his sister for a while and knew that God had called him into the ministry. He immediately stood up with no hesitation. I literally had to hold the sides of my chair to keep from doing the same. In that moment, as dozens of young men and women stood, I remained in my chair. While my body was seated, my heart was standing in defiance to God.

The speaker then asked if you were sitting next to someone who was standing, to hold up their arms as we prayed over them. We were symbolically going to be the Aaron and Hur for those who were called into the ministry. There I was, tears streaming down my face, holding up the right hand of my future brother-in-law, so proud of his call to the ministry, and at the same time, so ashamed of my own cowardly behavior.

The conference ended, Christmas break was over, and we headed back to school. I told no one of what had happened at the conference, and all outward signs were still pointing toward accomplishing *my* plan. My brother and I finished up our sophomore year of college, still on track for that degree in business and accounting. Sill headed toward our dream of owning a sporting goods store. Myself, continuing to run from the call God had placed on my life.

My brother got married in June and chose not to return to college the following semester. He had received a good job in our hometown and would be taking a semester off before returning to finish up his degree. This changed everything in my life. For the first time, I would be doing life without my brother by my side. I was happy for him. I was *thrilled* for him, actually. He married a great woman, and as far as I knew, he was walking in the will of God. But for me, it was one giant reminder that I was *not* in God's will.

I returned to school for my Junior year and jumped right back into those business and accounting classes, only this time something was different. Every second of every class those first two weeks of school were unbearable. I hated every moment. With the dawn of each new day, every stroke of a pencil to paper, turn of a page in a book, every night with my head on the pillow, all I could think about was not standing up at that conference.

I'm not sure I slept those first two weeks of my Junior year. I'm sure I did, but it felt as if I were up 24-7, wallowing in my shame, wondering if I could cut it as a pastor or even if God would let me after I denied Him once already. Finally, in the middle of the night, unable to sleep again, I got out of my bed, opened up my Bible, and started reading in Proverbs. I came to a verse that is now my "Life verse". I have this verse framed on the wall of my office as a constant reminder.

> **Many are the plans in a man's heart, but it is the Lord's purpose that prevails.**
>
> **(Proverbs 19:21 NIV 1984)**

It was as if God wrote that verse for me to read in that exact moment. I have never heard God's audible voice, but I've felt His voice in such a powerful way that I'm not sure audible could be any clearer. In that moment it was as if God was saying to me,

"Jeff, I'm not going to let you sleep until you surrender to this call. You might have all kinds of plans, but my purpose *will* prevail. I've called you into the ministry."

That was it. In that moment I surrendered to God's calling on my life. I didn't know what that fully meant at the time. I had no idea that the calling would eventually lead to me starting a church in Cheyenne, WY. If God had shown me that, I'm not sure I would have survived the night. At the very least, I would have needed a new pair of undershorts. All I knew was I had been called, and if I were to keep on denying that call, I would be living in outright sin against God.

The next day I went to my academic advisor and told him the whole story. I was attending a Christian liberal arts university, so he helped me do the work of changing my major to pastoral ministry, and changing the plan for my life. I then headed home for the weekend to tell my family what God was doing in my heart.

The enemy will play crazy tricks on you, by the way. He had convinced me that my dad would be mad about my calling. He'd already helped pay for two years of college and now I was changing directions mid stream. What would he say?

I was also convinced my brother would be angry since our plan was now essentially "down the drain." Of all the people who would be mad at me for choosing to obey the call of God, I think my dad and brother would be last on that list, but I was terrified to tell them.

In fear and trepidation, I shared the news with them. As only God can do, He silenced the mouth of the enemy and built me up through the support and encouragement of my family. My dad, my brother and my family were thrilled at what God was doing in me.

Back at school, I was now showing up in ministry classes and not showing up in the business ones. Questions quickly came up. Time and time again people asked, "Why are you not in class anymore?" or "Why are you in this class?" My answer then is my answer now… "Because I'm called!" I would tell them. "Because I'm called!"

My question for you is have you had that "youth conference" moment in your life? Do you need to stand up for the call? Has God confirmed something through His Word? Is there someone you need to tell? Whatever your next step is and no matter what God's asking you to do; you can let go of your seat, stand up for the call and tell the world. The plans you have made may be plenty, but you can *trust*, the Lord's purpose will prevail. That's good news … because you're called!

CHAPTER 7

Inception

We look to Jesus not to fulfill our shallow longings or provide for us creature comforts. We look to Him to lead us where He needs us most and where we can accomplish the most good. --- Erwin McManus in The Barbarian Way

Remember the movie *Inception*? GREAT film. For me, it was one of the most creative and visually stunning movies I'd ever seen. If you've seen the movie you'll remember, if you haven't, I'll fill you in.

The film centers around the idea that there are dreams within dreams; and you can even interject yourself into someone else's dream and plant thoughts in their subconscious. I won't get into all the ins and outs of the film, but it's the dream within a dream idea I want to focus on.

When it comes to our unique calling in life, we've got to remember that just like our sanctification, the call doesn't end with one surrender. Just like I shouldn't climb on the altar, give God my body, but never surrender anything else to Him in my life, neither do I follow God's call but then never surrender to any other "calls" within that call again.

Inside of the unique calling God's given you, there are going to be other calls that God places on your life. If you're an author, it might be the call to write another book. If you're a pastor, perhaps a call to a new congregation or ministry opportunity. If you're a stay-at-home mom, the call for more children, adoption, or maybe homeschooling your kids.

Whatever it is God has called you to, there will be "calls within the call." It's our response to those inner callings that will shape where God takes us in the unique calling that He has placed upon our lives.

I've seen this in my own life in a number of different ways. Whether it was the call to my first pastorate in Ringwood, OK, right out of college (The grace of those people toward me in that first congregation was *enormous*! The fact that they let a young punk like me minister to them is *so* humbling), to the call of God on us to move to Wyoming and lead a youth ministry. God has always been faithful to clearly reveal His "call within the call."

No calling has been more clear to me, though, than that of launching Element Church. Throughout my ministry, I always had a huge admiration for church planters. So many of the church planting stories I heard were filled with the kind of faith I thought I could never have and required charisma I knew I did not possess.

I remember telling people, "I could *never* plant a church. I don't have the gift mix for it!" I'm an introvert by nature. I'm very extroverted on the platform but very introverted in a room; especially in a room of people I don't know. I'm not the kind of guy that can walk into a room and learn everyone's name or story.

I walk into a room and hope no one asks my name or wants to know my story.

To plant a church, it seemed like God would need that outgoing, connecting, bubbly personality that has read *"How to win friends and influence people"* from cover to cover. I'm more of a "How to lose friends and tick off people" personality. Ok, maybe it's not that bad, but I was convinced God would *never* ask me to start a church. Why would he? I didn't fit the mold.

We were six years into serving as youth pastors in Gillette, WY, when God began to do something new in my heart. I loved the students we were leading. I loved the pastor whom I served under, the people of our church, and the community of Gillette itself. We were happy, comfortable and established. At the time, we had three kids, a great home provided for us by the church and a generous salary. There was no reason for us to desire anything to change. However, on January 10th of 2006, everything started to do just that.

I was sitting in my recliner that morning having my quiet time with God. I had finished reading my Bible and picked up the book I had been reading by Erwin McManus called, *"The Barbarian Way."* I had already been challenged, even convicted by the book, but nothing like what God was about to do from one statement.

On page 54 of The Barbarian Way, Erwin says this: **We look to Jesus not to fulfill our shallow longings or provide for us creature comforts. We look to Him to lead us where He needs us most and where we can accomplish the most good. --- Erwin McManus in *The Barbarian Way***

Those words pierced my heart like none of the other words in the book. It was as if God was using this book to give me a "call within a call". It was the beginning of another inception moment for me. I didn't know what the call was yet; I only knew that I needed to start praying.

I cried out to God; "Lord, I don't want to be so comfortable that I miss out on what you want me to do. If you want to do something new with my life, I'm willing. Whatever it is God; this is my prayer, 'Put me where I can do *You* the most good.' If that's staying here, I'll stay. If it's something new, I'll go."

Every day I began praying that prayer. "Put me where I can do you the most good." It's a prayer I challenge you to pray as well. It's the kind of prayer Pastor Derek prayed that opened the door to his calling. (Chapter 3) I call it a "dangerous prayer," because if you pray it, and listen closely, God will reveal His will for you. Then it's up to you to obey.

A couple of weeks into praying that prayer, I started to feel as if God was releasing us from our current ministry position and giving me a desire for something I didn't think I would ever do again: be the senior pastor of a church. So, my prayers turned to, "God, if you want to move us on to another congregation, I'm open to that. I just want *You* to put *me* where I can do *You* the most good."

I thought God was going to lead us down the "normal" path of many youth pastors. Open up a position at a small church that needed a senior pastor and begin a new ministry journey into senior leadership.

Small, however, didn't quite describe what God was about to call us to. "Nothing" would be a better description; because God began to stir my heart, and give me a love for a city I'd never been to and knew nothing about - Cheyenne, WY. This was odd because we didn't have a church of our denomination in

Cheyenne. It meant if God were calling us to Cheyenne, we would be starting something *new*!

I was terrified at that thought! I had literally never been to Cheyenne, except to stop for gas or food on the way to Denver. I knew nothing about the church landscape of the community. I didn't know what kind of churches were there or what kind of churches it needed. Again, I'm not the church planting type. "God, you've got the wrong guy," I said. "Are you sure you got the message to the right person? I mean, is there a 'Geoff' Maness out there somewhere? Because my name is spelled with a 'J'." But the message was for me. I couldn't shake this passion, this love for a city and a people I knew nothing about.

My wife was the only other person who knew about this stirring in my heart. She joined me in praying as we sought out God's clarity on this call. It was late February of 2006. I was again sitting in my chair one morning, having my quiet time with God, reading in Isaiah from the *NLT One Year Chronological Bible* and I threw out my fleece.

"Lord, if you want us to start a church in Cheyenne, you're going to have to make it *abundantly* clear. If this new thing is from You, I *have* to know." That's when I read Isaiah 43:18-19, which has become the foundational verses for our church.

> **"But forget all that --- it is nothing compared to what I'm going to do. For I am about to do a *brand-new thing*. See, I have already begun! Do you not see it? I will make a pathway in the wilderness for my people to come home. I will create rivers for them in the desert."**
>
> **(Isaiah 43:18-19 NLT 1st edition)**

This was one of those moments where I didn't hear an audible voice, but I can't imagine audible being any clearer than what God spoke to my heart. "Starting a church in Cheyenne is *your* brand new thing. It's where you can do *Me* the most good." I stopped my reading, looked up at my wife who was nearby and said, "Honey, we're moving to Cheyenne." She was on board 100-percent.

In the weeks following, God also confirmed His call through other people. I traveled to Rapid City, SD, to visit my Grandparents. I don't know any one more in tune with God's Spirit than them. They are saints in the highest sense of the word. I was sitting in their living room, talking about life, faith and ministry, when God used my Grandmother to speak a word of confirmation to my heart. She said, "Have you ever thought about planting a church? I think you'd be really good at that."

I'm glad I wasn't eating or drinking anything at that moment because I may have choked on it or spit it out. My eyes must have been as big as saucers and my mouth must have dropped to the floor. I said, "Grandma, you have no idea what you just spoke." I proceeded to tell her about God's *new thing* in my life.

Then the hard part came. How would I tell my pastor? I loved him. I could have worked for him for as long as I could imagine being in ministry. Not only did He love God, but he also genuinely loved me and cared for my family. I am certain I would not be the pastor or man I am today without his coaching and mentor relationship.

About a month after I'd committed to God that we would start a church in Cheyenne, I called our pastor on a Sunday afternoon and asked if I could come over to talk. Now that I'm a senior pastor, I realize that Sunday afternoon was probably the *worst* possible timing to have this conversation.

I arrived at his house, walked into his den and sat down beside him. There was no small talk to be had. My heart was about to pound out of my chest. Outside of my family and a few very close friends, *no one* knew about this new thing. "How will he respond?" I thought, "Will I even have a job next week?" Again, the enemy was trying to talk me out of doing this just like he did when I was first called to the ministry.

I blurted it out, "Dan, I feel like God's calling us to start a church in Cheyenne. I don't know how that looks, and it won't be for another year or so, but my time here at High Plains is coming to an end. I know that the church may not be able to help us out financially, but I *have* to go. This is what God has called us to do."

I prepared myself for the hurt and betrayal I would cause to be revealed on his face, but Dan just calmly said, "Ya know Jeff, a couple weeks ago God started preparing me for this. He just kept speaking to my heart that your time with us was coming to an end. I want you to know that *whatever* we can do for you as a church, we are behind you 100 percent."

Wow! Within the span of a few weeks God confirmed His calling through my spirit, His Word and some trusted relationships. The adventure was on! Little did I know in those early stages that seven years down the road, we'd see over a thousand souls won into the Kingdom, more than twelve hundred people attending our church each weekend, two campus' in the state of Wyoming, and a vision to impact the entire state.

I didn't see the marriages that would be restored, the addicts that would be set free, or the families that would be rebuilt. I didn't see the callings God would place on other people's lives through this ministry. I didn't see the outreach opportunities God would open up. I didn't know we would purchase and rebuild a duplex home for short-term affordable housing for families in need. I didn't see a staff with multiple full-time employees, and I definitely didn't see a book! All I saw was a call. "Cheyenne!" All I knew to do was obey. I'm so glad we did!

Early on in this process, I was having lunch with a friend. I was asked a very direct, but innocent question from them. One that revealed just how small my faith was in what God could actually do. They asked, "How big do you think Element Church will be?" I said, "Ever?" "Yeah," was their reply. Looking back, my answer to that question is embarrassing. I think my exact words were, "If we ever had five hundred people, I would poop my pants." We passed five hundred people about seven hundred people ago, and God is *definitely* not done!

He's not done with you either! No matter where you're at in life right now. No matter where you've been and no matter what you've done, God has a plan for you. It's never too late! As long as you're breathing, there is a purpose for your life, and my bet is you just took another breath.

You...yes *you*, are uniquely designed *by* God to live out a God-sized purpose *for* God. It may not be starting a church, but it's *your* calling, and God's trying to get it through to you. So what if you just started praying, "God, put *me* where I can do *You* the most good," and see what happens? Why? Because you're called.

CHAPTER 8

The cost of the call

Anything great done for God will come at the cost of something great!

If I didn't write this chapter in the book, I would be doing you an injustice. It would be easy to write about the great successes we've had as a church and I've had in this call, but if I didn't share the sufferings or the scars, I wouldn't be sharing the whole story. While I can honestly say that my calling has brought me some of the greatest pleasure in life, it has also caused some of my greatest pain.

The idea that our calling will not cost us something is a lie. I honestly believe it's why many people abandon the call when times get tough. No one told them about the hurt, the pain, the struggle, or the opposition. *Yes*, living out your calling is amazingly fulfilling, but you either have already, you are now, or you will go through times of great pain or problems. Anything great done for God will come at the cost of something great! In the middle of that cost, it's *only* the calling that will keep you committed.

If God has called you to something great, and any call from God is, then there will be some tests along the way; and those tests are usually in the form of a cost. Following God's call might move you away from family, it might require a pay cut, a career change, or to quote my son Jonah, "Moving to a place where there are wars." To think that God's call will make us *more* comfortable is both arrogant and American.

Comfort is often the enemy of our calling. I'm not saying you'll never be comfortable when living out God's call, but in order to fulfill our calling we will constantly be living on the edge of comfort and chaos. Whoever said, "The safest place to be is in the center of God's will," has obviously never been in the center of God's will. Oftentimes the most *dangerous* place to be is in the center of His will.

At some point and in some way, you're calling will be tested. There are probably more, but I believe the cost to our calling generally shows up in three tests: Opposition, opportunity and obligation. Inside these three tests are unlimited levels to the degree of the cost. Opposition from an obstinate church member is much different than opposition from the government in a country where Christianity is illegal. No matter the case, every cost and test, I believe, will fall into one of these categories.

The Cost: Part 1 --- Opposition

We served as youth pastors to a congregation in Gillette, WY, for almost 4 ½ years. In that time frame we purchased and remodeled an entire facility into a youth center for our growing ministry, and seemed to be making a real impact in the community. Overall, the church seemed to be going great as well. Attendance was solid, giving was fantastic and lives were being changed, when one Monday, my ministry life was flipped upside down.

Monday was my day off at the time, and we had taken our family out of town for the day. When we arrived back at the house late that evening the answering machine was flooded with messages about what had happened. Earlier in the day, our senior pastor had been forced to resign by a group of leaders within our denomination.

The way I still see it, there were *extreme* philosophical differences in ministry between them and our pastor. It was deemed "unhealthy" for him to remain the pastor of our church. This made no sense to me since all the signs of health seemed obvious.

I was devastated. It literally tore our church apart. We had just taken a congregational vote at our annual business meeting, and our pastor was elected to remain such with well over the required percentage necessary. This was by far the worst church experience I had or have ever had in my life. It definitely was *not* how I saw Jesus wanting His bride to act. I didn't know what to do, all I knew was I couldn't continue in this church.

The same week that the removal of our pastor was final, I tendered my resignation as the youth pastor. I still felt called to those students and to the community, but I could not side with the decision that was made. For me, it was a matter of standing up for what was right. I told those who made the decision, "How can I preach to our students every week about 'standing up for what's right no matter the cost' and not do the same in this situation?"

My heart was so grieved by what happened that I planned on taking a break from ministry altogether. I didn't know if I would ever go back to ministry. A large group of people who loved and supported our pastor had also decided they could not side with the decision that was made and had already started meeting together as a church body somewhere else. A facility was made available to them and many of our students were attending that new church as "sheep without a shepherd".

This new congregation asked our pastor, who was without a church, and myself, if we would stay in Gillette, and continue leading them in ministry. I didn't know what to do other than pray, and as I prayed God was abundantly clear, "This is where I've called you to be." So we said, "Yes!"

I had already been scheduled to speak at a youth camp while all this was going on, and didn't want what happened to keep me from this obligation, so I flew out to serve at the camp. While there I got a phone call from a representative of our denomination. They informed me that the leaders who had removed our pastor also were aware I had chosen to stay with the new congregation that was formed, and asked if I was *sure* I wanted to do that. I felt called, so I told them the only thing I knew to say; "I have to." I said, "I believe it's what God has called me to do."

I'll never forget what was said next. My actions were believed to be such an egregious breach of ethics, there was no other recourse but to remove my credentials. This was the denomination I had grown up in. I had never known another one. I went to the denominational school. I pastored in it. I was ordained in it. My Dad and my Grandpa were both ordained in this denomination. For me, this opposition was a test in the highest degree. I didn't know what else to say so I said, "Okay," and that was the end of our conversation.

Four and a half years of school, seven years of full-time ministry, a lifetime in this denomination, and my ordination was stripped, my credentials taken away. I didn't know what that meant, or what it would mean down the road. I knew I was most likely un-hirable now in the only denomination I'd ever known.

Not too long after that, my Grandpa (who is ordained in that same denomination) gave me a call. I hadn't received many phone calls from him in my life. Not that we don't have a good relationship, it was just phone calls from him weren't all that common. God used his voice that day, in the face of opposition, to confirm God's call on my life. Our conversation was brief, but *man* was it clear.

Grandpa read me a verse from the Bible that he felt God wanted me to hear. Then he said this: "Jeff, the 'denomination' (which he used by name) didn't ordain you, *God* ordained you and that cannot be taken away!" Wow! It was exactly what I needed to hear. God was not ultimately concerned about where I held my credentials; He was concerned about whether I was obedient to the call.

Your calling will be tested through opposition. That opposition will cost you something. For me, at the time, it was my credentials as a pastor. For you, it might be something much greater, or much more valuable. Looking back, it was that specific opposition which opened up the door for the opportunity to start Element Church.

We ended up joining another denomination, which even though my credentials had been revoked, graciously granted me ordination in their denomination as a transfer. Our new denomination has a real heart for church planting, and an incredible success rate to boot. I'm certain that outside of this opposition, the opportunity to start Element Church may not have ever been presented. I'm actually thankful now for the opposition I was required to face back then.

The Cost: Part 2 --- Opportunity

I know you don't normally think of "opportunity" as a test or a cost, but bear with me. Not too long after God called us to start Element Church, an opportunity was presented that was a *huge* test to our call. After we went public with God's calling to start a church in Cheyenne, the reality of what we were doing was beginning to set in. We had zero guarantees. We were leaving a healthy church, loving congregation, growing youth ministry, consistent paycheck and a perfect home, for what? Complete uncertainty.

We didn't know a soul in Cheyenne. We didn't have a church body, let alone a facility to meet in. We hadn't found a home. We were guaranteed a salary for the first year from our current church, but after that we were on our own. The cost of what we were about to do was staring us straight in the face. Whether this was a test from God or a temptation from the enemy I do not know, but at the exact time I was feeling the pressure and uncertainty of what we were about to do, I received an opportunity for something else.

A friend of ours, who knew we were called to Cheyenne, talked to me one day. It seemed like it was the day I was feeling the pressure the most. The offer was simple. Their church was not looking for a pastor *yet*, but they thought maybe they would be. Their pastor was possibly nearing the end of his ministry, and because of that, some of the people in their church were already looking for something new. Something fresh.

"If we can get our pastor to resign," this person said, "would you consider coming to our church?" It wasn't an "official" offer, but it peaked my curiosity for sure. The church in question was a *great* church. It was established. I didn't know the details, but from all appearances the salary would have been great, the housing even better, and the people were very loving. I thought very seriously about that offer.

At the time we had three kids with one on the way, and here we were, headed off into the most uncertain times of our lives. The potential cost of what we were doing was overwhelming. If this didn't work out, what would we do? My only skill was pastoring, and I wasn't sure I was that great at it. All my insecurities and every possible excuse came rushing to my mind. "If we quit now," I thought, "no one get's hurt."

I hung up the phone without giving an answer and turned up the radio to try and drown out the noise in my heart. Just as the timing on the phone call seemed impeccable, so was the song on the radio. It was Matt Redman's, *Blessed Be Your Name.* These were the lyrics I heard:

Blessed Be Your Name
In the land that is plentiful
Where Your streams of abundance flow
Blessed be Your name

Blessed Be Your name
When I'm found in the desert place
Though I walk through the wilderness
Blessed Be Your name

Blessed Be Your name
When the sun's shining down on me
When the world's 'all as it should be'
Blessed be Your name

Blessed Be Your name
On the road marked with suffering
Though there's pain in the offering
Blessed be Your name

I liked the sound of "abundance" and "plentiful". I liked the "sun shining on me" and "the world as it should be." But suffering?

Pain? Desert? Wilderness? It was as if God were saying, "Jeff, whether you have plenty or whether you are poor, that is not my calling for you. My calling is Cheyenne, and I'm asking you to go. Leave the provision up to Me, and praise Me no matter what."

I immediately turned down the "offer" my friend had made. It was an opportunity that was a test to my call and revealed the cost I had to be willing to make. Your calling will be tested through opportunity as well. The opportunity to make more money, take an easier route, move closer to home, work with a friend or have a better house.

There's nothing wrong with *any* of those things, by the way. In fact, I hope that in your calling you're able to do *all* of those things. But remember, just because there's an opportunity, even a good one, doesn't mean you're obligated to take it. Opportunity is not always God's will. In fact, opportunity is often opposed to God's will.

I learned something that day that has stuck with me throughout my time in leading Element Church: I'm okay with uncertainty; it's clarity that I need. God was abundantly clear: "I've called you to Cheyenne, just leave the details up to me."

The Cost: Part 3 --- Obligation

I was on the way to the home of one of our staff members, who also happened to be one of my closest friends, to have the hardest conversation of my life. There was a pit in my stomach, my mind seemed to be in a million places and my heart felt like it was in a million pieces. The cost of what happened the day before was almost too much for me to bear. I felt like I was one step away from calling it quits. I loved the city we were in. I loved the church that I led. I loved the people I got to do life with, but I didn't know if it was worth it any longer. So I called the only person I knew who understood what we had been through…I called my wife.

She was one of the few people who even knew what had happened the day before, and she was the only person who knew what I was on the way to do. I don't think the phone call surprised her one bit. She answered with no other words but, "Hey!" I hesitated, felt a lump in my throat, and through some tears choked out, "Tell me why I'm doing this again." Her reply will forever echo in my heart. It's what kept me going that day, and it's what keeps me going every day. "Because you're called," she said. "Because you're called."

We were two years into planting Element Church when I made the hardest leadership, ministry or personal decision I've ever made in my life; removing one of my closest friends from his position on our team.

When God called us to start Element Church, he was the first person I told after my wife and the first person I asked to join our team. God had called his family to leave everything behind as well, move to a new city, change their kids' schools, get new jobs, and be a part of this "new thing" God was doing.

The entire year before we planted Element, and the first two years of our ministry, there wasn't one decision, event, service or outreach he was not a part of. There was no doubt God had called him and his family to help start Element Church, and no doubt he was gifted for his launch team role.

Element Church was blessed with substantial and fast-paced growth from its opening day, and to be honest, it was growth we were not prepared for. I love what God has done in our church, but sometimes it feels like we grew too quickly. Or maybe we grew too quickly for what I had intentionally prepared us for. We did not structure ourselves for that kind of growth. (Perhaps another sign of my lack of faith)

There were no moral or ethical issues involved in my friend's dismissal. His integrity was never in question. But 18 months into our rapid growth, it was becoming clear to me that the leadership responsibility was outgrowing his leadership capacity. We tried switching up his responsibilities on the team, adjusting his role in the ministry to find his sweet spot, but it just wasn't working out.

At some point in our relationship, I stopped pushing him in leadership because I knew if I kept pushing, it would damage our friendship. Looking back, delaying the difficult conversations ended up damaging our relationship the most. I had failed him as a leader, and I had failed him as a friend.

Again, I won't go into all the details, and as always, each person involved will have their own side of the story, but a couple of years into our journey, everything had come to a head. Either I would be obligated to the call of God to lead this church forward, which meant removing him from his full time position of leadership, or I would be obligated to our relationship and hinder the church from moving forward as God desired.

I was a divided man to say the least. I knew where God was leading us as a church and what that meant for our team, but I also knew the incredible sacrifice he had made to join the team. I thought about the incredible commitment he had given to the call of God. I could tell stories of the incredible impact he had in our church and in our community.

He was a highly loved and well-respected part of our church body and team. He had deep relationships and powerful influence among our people. Relationally, he was an all star. I knew if we made the decision to remove him from the team, not only would it cause a chasm in our friendship, but potentially insurmountable damage to our church.

"What will people say? What if 'so and so' leaves? We can't afford to lose that giver! If I remove him from the team, it might destroy our church. If I remove him from the team, it will destroy our friendship!" Those thoughts, and many others, dominated my thoughts. I changed my mind by the minute leading up to this decision.

I had told our Executive Pastor that I knew what needed to be done for the calling of our church, but wasn't sure if I could make that decision due to the obligation of my friendship, and the fear of the potential fall out. Our Executive Pastor was more than patient with me during that time, as he continues to be to this day. He was clear, "Whatever you feel like we need to do, I'm with you."

I was praying for clarity. Would I be obligated to the call of God or to my friendship? Sadly, those two obligations will often collide, and when they do the cost is enormous. I knew what God was calling me to do, but I didn't know if I could do it or if it was worth the cost.

One day, I was having my quiet time with God, when I read the story of King Saul not fully following through on everything God had called him to do. He had defeated the Amalekites, but not completely destroyed them as God had commanded. He kept the best for himself and for the people. The prophet Samuel confronted Saul on his disobedience to the call of God, and King Saul ends up saying this in **1 Samuel 15:24**:

> **Then Saul admitted to Samuel, "Yes, I have sinned. I have disobeyed your instructions and the**

> **LORD's command, for I was afraid of the people and did what they demanded. (NLT)**

I immediately stopped. That was me! I was living in the fear of men more than the fear of God. I was putting more faith in people than I was in Him. God had made Himself clear. The obligation to the call *had* to be greater than my obligation to men. I immediately told our Executive Pastor what I felt needed to be done. A few days after my decision had been made; my friend was removed from his full-time position on our team.

The next day, I drove over to his house to talk with him personally about what had taken place. This was when I called my wife. The hurt was deep. The pain was sharp. The cost was unbearable. I knew our relationship would never be the same, and it's not.

I would still call him a friend today, but nothing like it was before. It's more cordial than committed. He is currently attending and volunteering in another congregation, and I believe God is using him to accomplish more good now than he ever could have full-time on our team.

Obligation will be a test to your calling. Your obligation to the call might cost you a relationship, it might cost you some comfort or it might cost you your life. In that moment, and in the moment of every test I've faced, it seemed like the cost would never be overcome.

When I was opposed, I thought my ministry was over. When I received an opportunity, I believed my family would not be provided for. When I faced divided obligations, I was convinced I would destroy the church. Now, years later, leading a church larger than I ever imagined, headlong into a building expansion, starting an additional campus & scores of life change later, I'm beginning to learn, the call is *so much bigger* than the cost.

When opposition arises or opportunity is presented, when obligation forces the hardest decision of your life, and it will: it's *God's call* that will keep you committed in the face of *great cost.* Anything great done for God will come at the cost of something great! Be ready for the cost…because you're called.

CHAPTER 9

I thought I saw a Kangaroo

When it seems like God is preventing you from seeing a dream fulfilled, it might be that He's preparing to fulfill the dream through you!

I know that someone could be reading this thinking, "I know what God has called me to do. He's already placed a dream in my heart, but all I've done is wait." For many people the distance between what is current and what is called seems to be forever. You've lived in a state of limbo for years. Maybe it's a dream to be a mom, a desire to start a business or a vision to plant a church. Whatever it is, God's given it, but you've yet to see it. If that's you, then this is your chapter.

Sometimes it feels like God is preventing us from accomplishing the very thing He placed within us. That's where we need to understand this: When it seems like God is preventing you from seeing a dream fulfilled, it might be that He's preparing to fulfill the dream through you!

I'll never forget the time we were driving down a two-lane stretch of highway in the middle of nowhere Wyoming, when all of the sudden my wife gasped, and said quite loudly, "*Whoa*! *Whoa*!" I, of course, thought we were about to get run over by an 18-wheeler, slammed by a herd of antelope or were headed toward a little old lady walking across the highway.

I immediately hit the brakes, felt my heart leap, looked around frantically and said, "*What*?" "Oh, nothing," she replied softly. "*Nothing*? You can't say 'nothing' when you just yelled as if we were about to die. What was it?" "Nothing," she said again. As any good husband would do, I did *not* let this go. I had to find out why my wife gasped as we were driving down the highway. Finally, I had bugged her long enough that she let the cat out of the bag.

"I thought I saw something," she said. "Okay? What did you see?" She looked down, quieted her voice and sheepishly said, "I thought I saw a kangaroo." "A kangaroo?" I said. "We're in Wyoming…the *middle* of Wyoming. Why would there be a kangaroo?" She didn't have an answer, so I asked a clarifying question. "Well, what did you really see?" Her reply? "An antelope."

As we were driving down Hwy 59 in the middle of Wyoming, she spotted something out of the corner of her eye. Her immediate reaction told her it was a kangaroo, but upon further inspection, and a split second more of time, her perspective revealed the truth. It was not a kangaroo, but an antelope. Perspective changes everything. It really does. Enter Sarai.

In Genesis chapter 15, the Lord makes a covenant promise to Abram. He tells him that even though he is old in age and yet to have any children, God will provide through him an heir with descendants as numerous as the stars in the sky. This had to be an overwhelming and far-fetched idea for Abram and Sarai. They were already well advanced in years, and the idea of children for them was far behind.

In Genesis chapter 16, Sarai had waited long enough. The unfulfilled dream was too much to bear, so she took matters into her own hands.

> **Genesis 16:1-2** records: **Now Sarai, Abram's wife, had not been able to bear children for him. But she had an Egyptian servant named Hagar. So Sarai said to Abram, "The Lord has *prevented* me from having children. Go and sleep with my servant. Perhaps I can have children through her." And Abram agreed with Sarai's proposal.**

The dream had been given *by* God, but Sarai wasn't willing to wait *for* God. Quite honestly, neither was Abraham. Not his greatest moment of husbandly leadership here. Sarai believed God was preventing her from seeing the dream fulfilled, when in reality he was just preparing to fulfill the dream through her.

You may know the rest of the story. Abram did what his wife suggested. He slept with Hagar who then bore him a son named Ishmael. Sarai ends up despising Ishmael, expels him and Hagar from the family, and Ishmael became the father of just about every enemy nation the Israelites would ever know. Forcing the call of God always results in further chaos. Abram and Sarai are proof of that.

In chapter 21 of Genesis, we read about the miraculous conception and birth of the child of the promise. Isaac was born to Abraham and Sarah when he was 100 and she, 90. The promise had been fulfilled, but not without a price.

Division, enmity, strife and war had been brought into the family because of their lack of patience. What Sarah thought God was preventing *from* her, He was actually preparing just *for* her. Her perspective needed to change. She thought the dream was impossible *for* her, but God wanted to accomplish the impossible *through* her, she just needed to wait. Sarai could have learned a lot from the patience of Nehemiah, and so can we.

In Nehemiah chapter 1, he received a vision from God to go rebuild the walls of Jerusalem. He had heard in a report that the walls of his hometown were destroyed and the city was in ruins. God used this news to ignite a call on Nehemiah's life. There were two problems: He wasn't living in Jerusalem, and he was not an expert in building walls.

At the time, Nehemiah was the cupbearer to King Artaxerxes of Persia. How did he respond when he received the call of God? He waited. He waited for *God's* opportunity. He waited for an open door. In the meantime, he was the best cupbearer possible. He waited well. He fasted. He prayed. He praised. He worked a career until God opened the door for his call. It was in the *meantime* that God was making the way for a *miracle*.

God eventually opened the door for Nehemiah to go. Not only was Nehemiah allowed to go back to Jerusalem, but King Artaxerxes also wrote letters to the governors of all the regions he would be passing through. Those letters instructed the governors to give Nehemiah safe passage. They also informed the managers of the king's forest to give him timber, which would be used in rebuilding the gates. If that wasn't enough, the king also sent along army officers and horsemen to protect him. What was the end result? Because Nehemiah was willing to *wait*, God was able to do a *work*. The walls were eventually rebuilt in just fifty-two days.

Sometimes, the best thing you can do when you're called is wait; but choose to have patience like Nehemiah. Wait well! Don't complain about your situation. Don't whine about your position. Don't worry about how God's going to fulfill the dream. Just wait. When it seems like God is preventing you from seeing a dream fulfilled, it might be that He's preparing to fulfill the dream through you!

Or what about Joseph? Joseph was given dreams that weren't fulfilled for decades. Waiting wasn't all that Joseph had to do either; he was also forced to wander. Thrown into a pit by his brothers and left to die, he was then sold into slavery where he was taken to Egypt, falsely accused by his master's wife of sexual assault, put into prison for a crime he did not commit and left with no hope of a pardon. Years later, he *was* released from prison and placed 2nd in command of Egypt just below Pharaoh. All of these things Joseph faced before he ever saw his dreams fulfilled.

Why was Joseph allowed to wander and then forced to wait for his dreams to be fulfilled? Didn't God have the ability to give Joseph the dream, fulfill it on the spot, and spare him all the hurt, pain and suffering? "Why all the waiting, God?" That's what I've asked on more than one occasion. "Why did You give me this dream if all You're going to do is delay?"

Psalm 105:19 Until the time came to fulfill his dreams, the Lord tested Joseph's character.

Whoa! The first time I truly *saw* that verse; it changed my perspective on everything. God's more concerned about my character than He is my calling. Sometimes He makes me wait because He's working on my character. Other times He makes me wait because He's working on a miracle. I know there are times

He makes me wait and I'll never know why, because His ways are higher than my ways, and His thoughts are higher than mine.

That's where it comes back to trust. It's in the waiting we've got to trust that God is working. Maybe he's working on *you.* Perhaps he's working on the place you will *go.* He might be working on the people you will meet. He could be working on your miracle. I don't know what He's working on right now, but when it feels like God is preventing you from seeing a dream fulfilled, it might be He's just preparing to fulfill the dream through you. We wait, but with a new perspective.

Nehemiah waited, and God opened the door to rebuild a city. Joseph waited, and God opened the door to rescue his entire family. Sarah refused to wait, opened the door herself and ended up with deep regret. What she thought God was preventing her from, He was actually preparing just for her - a miracle!

Don't miss out on the miracle just because you feel like you're missing out. If God has placed it in you, He will be faithful to fulfill it through you. Wait…because you're called.

CHAPTER 10

Do I have what it takes?

Often times God chooses to stack the odds AGAINST us so that when He comes through, NONE of the credit goes to us!

My prayer for this book has been that God would confirm or create callings in people's lives. I'm praying for an awakening to the reality that every one of us are uniquely designed *by* God to fulfill a God-sized purpose *for* God.

I believe right now, God has laid before each of us a task He wants us to accomplish, an assignment He wants us to complete, or a calling on our lives. The callings can be diverse. Perhaps you're being asked to face a difficult situation with dignity. Maybe you're being called to spiritually lead your family. It could be that you're being led to walk by faith and start a ministry, volunteer in your church, have a difficult conversation, make a financial sacrifice or head out into the mission field.

Whether it's a calling to change how you live or to change what you do for a living; I don't know what it is God's asking you to do, but I *do* know we all have something. When it comes to that something, if you're anything like me, you'll ask this question: "Do I have what it takes?"

The short answer is "*Yes*!" You *do* have what it takes, but just me saying that doesn't breed much confidence. I want to tell you how you can be *confident* you have what it takes, and I don't know of a better example in the Bible to prove this to you than Gideon.

Gideon is known for being a mighty warrior. He was a man of great courage and strength. He didn't start out that way, however. When we first read about Gideon in the Bible, he is anything but mighty and somewhere short of a warrior. If you're feeling apprehensive about what God is calling you to do, then Gideon is the perfect place to look for the proof that you will have what it takes.

In Judges chapter 6, Israel was many years removed from having their escape from slavery in Egypt and had moved into the Promised Land. This period of history is called the period of "the Judges". The people of Israel were going through cycles of disobedience *to* God, being banished *from* God to foreign countries, and then being rescued *by* God through leaders called "Judges". This cycle of disobedience, banishment and rescue continued for a very long time.

In chapter 6, the Israelites had once again been handed over to a foreign country, the Midianites, because of their disobedience. They were stripped of their grain, produce, and livestock. They even had their own people stolen or destroyed. By the time Israel cried out to the Lord for help, they were reduced to starvation. The Lord heard their cry, and responded:

> **The angel of the Lord came and sat down under the oak in Ophrah that belonged to Joash the Abiezrite, where his son Gideon was threshing**

wheat in a winepress to keep it from the Midianites. When the angel of the Lord appeared to Gideon, he said, "The Lord is with you, mighty warrior." (Judges 6:11-12 NIV)

If you don't think God has a sense of humor, you need to read that again. Gideon, who would later lead the army of Israel to defeat 135,000 soldiers of Midian with only 300 men of his own, was hiding in a winepress, threshing wheat because he was afraid the Midianites would take it.

To thresh wheat in that day you had to lay it on a cloth, pound it to break apart the chaff from the kernels, and then bounce the cloth so that the chaff would blow away in the wind leaving the desired kernels of wheat. If you were standing in a winepress, where the walls were big enough to stand inside and hide, how would the wind blow the chaff away?

Read those verses again, only with the image in your mind of Gideon standing in a winepress, hiding because he was scared, no wind inside the walls, tossing wheat into the air, only to have it all land back on him again and again. It must have felt like the most futile process. The angel of the Lord appeared and said, "The Lord is with you… mighty warrior!" Really?

You don't have to read much of the Bible to realize that because of the people God chose to use, God can use *you*! On the day Saul was being presented as the King, they found him hiding among nearby baggage. Moses ran away to the wilderness from his mistakes. Noah was way too old to accomplish any good. David was too young and an adulterer. Peter was unschooled, selfish and cowardly. Paul tried to destroy the church and Gideon was stuck in a winepress with wheat all over his face.

You may be reading this book, sitting in a winepress of your ow with wheat all over your face, and God is speaking to you - "Th Lord is with you, *mighty warrior*!"

Here is a truth we need to understand if we're going to be confident we have what it takes. The Lord sees who you *can* be, not just who you currently *are*. The Lord sees where you *will* be, not just where you're currently *at*. The Lord sees what you're *capable* of, not just what you're currently *doing*.

Wherever God finds you now is exactly where you need to be, He's just not going to let you stay there. God was about to ask Gideon to get out of his winepress, and maybe He is about to ask you to get out of yours. Know this: Wherever God asks you to go; He's put within you the ability to get there. Whatever God asks you to do, He's put within you the gifts to accomplish it. Whoever God asks you to be, He's already given you the strength to become.

God sees *in* you what you don't have the ability to see. "The Lord is with you, *mighty warrior*!"

To the young woman being pressured by a man to give something that doesn't belong to him until you say, "I do": "The Lord is with you, *mighty warrior*!"

To the man who is battling an addiction to pornography, sexual sin or temptation that seems to be overwhelming: "The Lord is with you, *mighty warrior*!"

To the parent whose children have made bad decisions, walked away from God and you're dealing with the pain, the hurt, and the doubt of who you are as a parent: "The Lord is with you, *mighty warrior*!"

o the couple facing marital conflict, financial stress, relational ncertainty and life's darkest hours: "The Lord is with you, *mighty warriors*!"

To the student whose "friends" are trying to take you down a path you know you don't want go: "The Lord is with you, *mighty warrior*!"

To the people who are called to do something you've never done, go somewhere you've never gone, be someone you've never been, or start something you never imagined and you're facing *huge* levels of uncertainty and fear: "The Lord is with you, *mighty warrior*!"

Do you believe it? Maybe you'll believe me if I say it this way: "You *are* a mighty warrior *because* the Lord is with you." That'll preach right there. Someone needs to hear that. Someone needs to read that. Someone needs to know that. Most importantly, someone needs to live that. This world needs more followers of Jesus who *know* who they are *because* of who is with them.

"The Lord is with you, *mighty warrior*!" It might sound as humorous to say to you as it did to Gideon, but God is not laughing. When God's people get serious about doing what He's called them to do, and being whom He's called them to be, the devil won't be laughing either. The last thing the devil wants is God's people believing that *He* is with them, because when we start believing God is with us, we'll start acting like mighty warriors.

Notice how Gideon responded. I wonder if this isn't how I often respond?

> **"Pardon me, my lord," Gideon replied, "but if the Lord is with us, why has all this happened to us?**

> **Where are all his wonders that our ancestors told us about when they said, 'Did not the Lord bring us up out of Egypt?' But now the Lord has abandoned us and given us into the hand of Midian." (Judges 6:13 NIV)**

This is *so* huge. The angel says, "The Lord is with you, mighty warrior," and Gideon didn't say, "Who, me?" Gideon didn't question the warrior part. Instead he challenged whether God was with him or not. "*If* the Lord is with us then *why* has all this happened to us?" I wonder if our doubts aren't actually in ourselves, as much as they are in God?

Why is it that we often equate difficulty with distance from God? Where if things aren't going our way then God must not be with us? Could it be that difficulty actually guarantees God's presence? When in the Bible did God ever give someone an easy job? Is there any Bible story where the main character had smooth sailing throughout their calling?

Every story we teach our children, every sermon illustration we use, we present the people who faced trials; hardship, persecution, temptation, loss, difficulty and we celebrate how God was *with* them as they walked *through* them. However, when difficulty comes *our* way, we assume God's not with us?

It's almost as if we think, "Well, I *could* do this, if God were with me." You have what it takes, not because of *you*, but because of God *with* you and *in* you. Check this out:

> **Now all glory to God, who is able, through his mighty power at work *within us*, to accomplish infinitely more than we might ask or think. (Ephesians 3:20 NLT)**

God's work is not most powerful outside of us but *inside* of us. We have *His* power in us to face what we need to face, do what we need to do, go where we need to go and be who we need to be. You might feel like you're in a winepress with an army preparing to attack, but the Lord is *with* you mighty warrior! Not only that, He's *in you!* That changes everything!

Gideon questioned God's presence, and this was God's response:

> **The Lord turned to him and said, "*Go* in the strength you have and save Israel out of Midian's hand. Am I not sending you?" (Judges 6:14 NIV)**

I love it! "Go in the strength you have." God told Gideon, and He's telling you today, the strength you already have is *all* the strength you need because it's not depending on your strength in the first place. Whatever it is God's asking you to do…*go* in the strength you have.

For some people, all you needed to hear in this book was, "*Go*!" You've been planning, you've been praying, you've been polishing your "call" for too long, and it's simply time to *go*! For others, you're letting your past keep you from your purpose. You think it's too late to follow God's call, but it's time for you to *go*!

Do you realize there are times that "Go!" is all God is going to say? Notice, God didn't tell Gideon how this would all work out, who would go with him, when it would be completed or even where he was supposed to go. He just said, "Go!" All throughout the Bible, God told His people to "Go!"

> **The LORD had said to Abram, "*Go* from your country, your people and your father's household to the land I will show you. (Genesis 12:1 NIV)**

> **So now, *go.* I am sending you to Pharaoh to bring my people the Israelites out of Egypt."**
>
> **(Exodus 3:10 NIV)**

> **After a long time, in the third year, the word of the LORD came to Elijah: "*Go* and present yourself to Ahab, and I will send rain on the land."**
>
> **(1 Kings 18:1 NIV)**

Again and again God says, "Go!" Even the Great Commission in Matthew chapter 28 says, "*Go* and make disciples…" Gideon however, protested:

> **"Pardon me, my lord," Gideon replied, "but how can I save Israel? My clan is the weakest in Manasseh, and I am the least in my family."**
>
> **(Judges 6:15 NIV)**

Other versions say, "but Lord" in place of "pardon me." Isn't that often our response? "But Lord." Like Gideon, we love to give God all the reasons why we can't do, can't go, can't be; as if we're going to change His mind based on our excuses. "But Lord, I can't afford to quit my job and start a new career." "But Lord, I can't talk to them about my faith, they hate the church." "But Lord, what if no one goes with me." "But Lord, but Lord, but Lord."

It's almost as if we expect God to say in surprise, "You're right! I hadn't thought of that! Well, if you really feel like you're not gifted in that area, can't afford to do it, your family won't like it, your friends might get angry, no one will go with you, or the odds aren't in your favor, then you better not go!"

It's easy to go when the odds are in our favor! The fact is, we often use odds as a measuring rod to determine whether God said,

Go." It's almost as if the less risky it is, the more safe and omfortable we feel, then the more we believe it's God's will.

We even pray for God to stack the odds in our favor, but God actually stacks the odds *against* us at times. Often times God chooses to stack the odds *against* us so that when He comes through, *none* of the credit goes to us! God doesn't always give us the details of how it'll all work out because He's looking for us to obey Him no matter what.

When God says, "Go," He means *go*; not "Go, unless you can show me something I haven't seen yet." God sees all, knows all, has thought of it all, and He's still choosing you to *go*! You might be waiting for God to give you something He's not going to give, or do something He's not going to do until you simply *go* in the strength you already have.

Now here is God's final response to Gideon's hesitation.

> **The Lord answered, "I will be with you, and you will strike down all the Midianites, leaving none alive." (Judges 6:16 NIV)**

I love this. So often this is how God works. Gideon says, "How am I going to save Israel from the Midianites?" God's answer is "*Me*!" God didn't give him the how, but rather, He gave him the *Who*. "I will be with you and you will strike down all the Midianites."

As far as Gideon knew, God was literally only going to use *him* to win the battle. Gideon wanted proof, but God gave him a new perspective. Gideon wanted a plan, but all he got was a different point of view. God said, "You want proof? You want a plan? Your plan is Me, and your proof is My presence. I will be with you, and that's all you need to know!" Sometimes the only thing

you'll have is God because He's trying to show you that He is a
you need!

"I will be with you," is all God told Gideon and it may be all He's going to tell you! "I will be with you. I am bigger than your circumstances. I am greater than your surroundings. I am stronger than your strongest strengths, and I cannot be stopped by your weakest weaknesses. I will overcome your excuses and overpower your enemies. I am all you need. I am with you, so *go*!"

How do I know you have what it takes? Because God is with you mighty warrior and… because you're called!

CHAPTER 11

Redefining Success

Success is not determined by the outcome but by our obedience to God.

I think it's time to redefine success when describing our calling. The idea of success is a really dangerous thing. It's dangerous because you can always find people, churches, organizations, businesses, etc., not doing as "well" as you are, which can lead to pride. You can also find people, churches, organizations, businesses, etc., that are doing things "better" than you are, which leads to defeat. When it comes to the outcome, there will *always* be people who are doing "better" than you and there will *always* be people you are doing better than. It just depends on which direction you're looking, and it's dangerous.

What's the measurement of better anyway? For me in the church world, better is almost always attendance. "That church has so many more people than we do. Why are we not as 'successful' as they are?" Or, "We are so much bigger than that church. We are way more 'successful' than they are."

This happens in parenting when we compare our children. happens in business when we compare profits or customers. Th happens in education when we compare grades and awards. Comparison happens everywhere, and it starts when we try to measure our success by the outcome.

Just because a church has more people than another, does it make them more successful? How many mega church pastors have we seen in the last decade be exposed in sexual immorality? Are they still a success? How many multi-billion dollar businesses or investment firms have been caught cheating the system? Are they still successful? Just because something or someone has all the *appearance* of success does not make them successful.

This game of chasing success is exhausting. I've been there as a pastor. I've gone through seasons where I've based my success on the weekend attendance. When I do that, I can be exhilarated one Monday and depressed the next. I'm up one week and down the next. I'm ready to charge the gates of hell with a water pistol, then I believe hell has conquered our church and I'm looking for a pistol.

Don't get me wrong; I *love* when our church is packed on a Sunday. We want to reach as many people as we can with Life in Christ. However, when I start to base success on the weekend numbers alone, I start aiming at the wrong thing. I might eventually hit the target, but I'll discover that it's not what I was ultimately looking for.

My entire perspective changed on success when I read 1 Kings chapter 2, a couple of years ago. In 1 Kings 2, David was nearing the end of his life on earth, and he was in the process of passing the baton of leadership to his son Solomon. Solomon was about to become king of Israel, and these were David's final words to him. In his charge to Solomon, King David said this:

> **"I am going where everyone on earth must someday go. Take courage and be a man." Observe the requirements of the Lord your God, and follow all his ways. Keep the decrees, commands, regulations, and laws written in the Law of Moses so that you will be *successful* in all you do and wherever you go. (1 Kings 2:2-3)**

It appears that David told Solomon, "*If* you obey, you *will* be successful," right? Don't we like that view of God? That's kind of a karma God, or a vending machine God. If I put the right stuff in, I'll get the right stuff out. We like that because we can leverage God that way. "Alright God, I obeyed, now give me my success." And again, what do we believe success is? *Outcomes*! More money, bigger churches, better businesses and perfect kids.

I have to admit, when I first read this, I thought, "What am I *not* doing that other pastors *are* doing? Are they obeying more than me so they get bigger churches, more speaking opportunities, better book deals?" DANGER! DANGER! DANGER! We must run from this kind of thinking when it comes to our call.

This is what God taught me the day I read this, and it forever changed my calling. I don't think David was telling Solomon, "Obedience will *bring* you success." I think David was telling Solomon, "Obedience *is* your success." "Solomon, *if* you obey God, you *are* successful. No matter what the outcome is, in all you do and wherever you go, you will be successful *because* you obeyed God." That's *huge*! It changes *everything*!

It's not an excuse to be lazy. It's not an option to only pray small prayers, dream small dreams, accomplish small tasks, or take fewer risks. It's actually the opposite. When success is not based on the outcome but on our obedience to God; I'm willing to do more, try harder, pray bigger, dream larger and risk greater! This liberating in our call.

It means it's not about *what* you do for God, it's about *if* you do what He's asking you to do. If you do what God's asking you to do with the best you can offer, you *are* successful in *all* you do!

Pastor: Preach boldly, lead courageously, love deeply and care compassionately.

Parent: Set boundaries, discipline Biblically, love unconditionally, spend time regularly and pray for earnestly.

Business owners: Treat people fairly, lead honorably, serve faithfully, and pay generously.

I could go on and on, but the key message is: Success is not determined by the *outcome* but by our *obedience* to God.

This changed my life so much, we made it the #1 core value of our church. We teach it, display it and do our best to live it. I haven't always lived it out perfectly, even since God challenged me from this passage. I still fight the temptation to measure success by outcome.

Just recently, I had to apologize to our leadership team for a decision I made that most people would consider a "small" one, but I went against the voice of God. I made a decision based on an outward sign of success instead of the inward success of obedience. The outcome actually "appeared" successful, but on the inside I knew it was not. It was a great reminder of whom I am working for. I work for the eyes of God alone! That's why obedience *must* be my success.

t the end of the day, I don't want to know I've accomplished reat things. I want to know I have obeyed my great God. God doesn't say, "Well done, my good and *successful* servant," but, "Well done, my good and *faithful* servant."

Fruitfulness is not the ultimate goal; faithfulness is. When I'm *faithful* to the call of God, I'll produce the *fruit* He is looking for. Is it time for you to redefine success? You should…because you're called!

CHAPTER 12

My Hero

Growing up, I lived with my hero. I want my family to live with theirs, and I want your family to live with theirs too!

I was blessed to be in a family where the pursuit of the call was always on display. I believe there is no greater example of obedience to the call than my dad. Yes, my dad had weaknesses. Yes, my dad failed on more than one occasion. Yes, he had to ask for forgiveness from God and also from his wife and kids. However, one thing you could not argue about my dad was his surrender to his calling.

My dad *was* and *is* my hero. A lot of people complain when someone compares them to their parent. They view it as a put down. While I did get my dad's dashingly handsome looks, I have also picked up some of his less positive traits. However, when people tell me, "You remind me so much of your dad," my heart swells with pride. My dad taught my siblings and I so much about the call, just by the way he lived. I want to share those things here in this final chapter.

There are *tons* of things I could share about my dad, but here are five things I learned about the call from watching my dad live his life. I hope they will help drive home the purpose and point (this book into your heart.

#1 The *first* call is to your family.

I know I've probably waited way to long to bring this up in a book on calling, but I was saving it for this chapter. If we're not careful, the idea of a call and doing something great *for* God can actually *become* our God. We can be so moved, so inspired, so "called" by God to do something that we pursue *it* at the expense of our family. Don't pursue the call of God so much that the call *becomes* your god.

After your relationship with Jesus, your calling to your family is number one. I never once questioned where the loyalties of my dad were. He was called to be a pastor, but his life showed that he was first called to be my dad (Or for my mom, her husband). My dad modeled his commitment to God, then his wife and kids, long before his commitment to the church.

I remember my dad using his days off to rotate taking us kids out individually for breakfast to his favorite hole in the wall called "The Busy Bee" in Buffalo, WY. I remember him playing offense/defense (a football game we made up) and hotbox (a baseball game) in the back yard too many times to count. I'm not sure he ever missed a ball game we had or a concert we were in, even though they must have been brutal at times to watch.

The memories I have of my dad are him with *me,* not him at the church. My only memories of him at the church are when I was there, tagging along, watching him love God and love people. His calling never became his mistress in our family. He loved the church, and he loved his call, but his calling to our family was his first priority. Yes, there were seasons where the call took more of is time than normal, but I honestly don't remember one of them. t's a testament to how committed he was to our family.

Not too long ago, our kids were talking about college and what they wanted to be when they grew up. They asked where they would live when they got a job. At this point, I made it clear they were *not* going to live with us forever. Then my daughter Mariah said this, "When I grow up I want to work in Wyoming, so that I can be a part of Element Church." Not just Cheyenne but Wyoming!

I *loved* hearing that. It meant she had already caught the vision of one church in multiple locations all across the state. But more importantly, it revealed that *maybe* I was starting to follow in my dad's footsteps. The fact Mariah wanted to be a part of our church years down the road meant she didn't resent my passion for it now. One of my bucket list items is that I would lead my family in such a way that when my kids are adults they will love Jesus and love His Church! They won't love the Church though if I place my calling to it before my commitment to them.

#2 The call is *not* about the money!

Ever! If someone tells me, "I feel called to do this or that… to go here or there, *but*…," I usually know what's coming next. "…*but* it doesn't pay very well." Call and pay don't mix. There is no amount of money on this planet that can satisfy a person's heart like living in the call of God.

My dad *never* went to a church for money, or *stayed* at a church for money. I know multiple times he took pay cuts to go where he was called. I know people questioned him on occasion saying, "Why would you do that?" I know there were times my dad didn't want to know the salary package of a church who was calling him because he didn't want that to affect His decision. His decision was based on the call of God alone! If you're called to i it is *not* about the money.

#3 The call has *one* opinion.

If you are pursuing a "call" because someone you admire is doing it, someone told you you'd be good at it, or you are feeling pressure from someone who has authority in your life, you are headed down a dangerous road. Don't enter a career or attempt a "call" because of the opinion of men. People who attempt a call for the sake of men will be the ones who eventually adjust the call for them as well.

There isn't a human on this planet that should change, manipulate or maneuver what I'm called to do. *Yes*, I understand we need to come under authority. *Yes*, I understand we might work for someone else in our career that also happens to be where we're called, but understand, there is no human opinion that matters when it comes to the call of God. The Apostle Paul put it this way:

> **As for me, it matters very little how I might be evaluated by you or by any human authority.**
> **(1 Corinthians 4:3 NLT)**

I'd be lying if I said human opinions don't weigh on my heart and mind. I want people to like me. I want them to think I'm a good leader. I want them to believe in what I'm doing. But you know what? When it comes down to it, I could care less about how I might be evaluated by any human. God will examine me and decide. This should drive what we do in *every* area of life, calling or not!

I saw, and quite honestly still see in my dad an unwavering commitment to the call of God and not any human opinion. I remember times when some of his closest friends would say things that hurt him deeply about decisions he made to follow the call. I know he received fall out for messages he preached, ministries he started, moves he made and people he confronted, all as part of trusting in God's opinion alone!

My dad received praise and honor from people too, but I believe he even took that with a grain of salt. You have to; otherwise you'll begin seeking the praise of men instead of giving praise to God by the way you live before men.

When you follow the call of God, people will pick you apart, question your every move and doubt your ability to lead. They will praise you in one moment and point their finger in disgust the next. It's in these moments of praise and finger pointing that we must trust in *one* opinion. Paul sure seemed to get this right.

2 Corinthians 6:8 We serve God whether people honor us or despise us, whether they slander us or praise us. (NLT)

I saw this modeled by my dad. Even when his own family doubted his decisions, my dad followed the call! Whatever God has called you to do and wherever He has called you to go, there is only *one* opinion that matters.... listen to it alone!

#4 The call is *tough.*

I don't think I realized this until I was in ministry, but now looking back, I can see how tough it was on my dad.

I remember one time in high school coming home late from a date with Sabrina (my eventual bride). It was definitely past my dad's normal bedtime and probably past my curfew, so as I pulled up and saw him sitting on the front porch I thought, "Uh oh, I'm in for it now." As I walked up to him though, I could tell he wasn't there for a conversation with me. He was having conversation with God.

I found out later that God was stirring something in his heart for a call to a new church in a new town, and he couldn't sleep. I know it had to be one night of *many* that God's calling kept him awake at night.

I remember demanding and critical people in my dad's life. I remember beginning to understand how closely watched our family was because "We were called". There are probably too many times to count when my dad and mom had conversations I never knew about when they discussed how *tough* the call was, but he never stopped living it out.

I know I'm not painting a pretty enough picture for some people about the call. I say these things because every time I go through a tough time, I'm reminded that if my dad can go through it, I can too. The call is tough, but if you're called, what else are you going to do? The tough parts of the call, at least for me, are far easier to endure than the emptiness in my heart of not following it!

#5 The Call is *unbelievable*!

Following the call of God is unbelievable! I don't know another word to describe it. I cannot imagine doing *anything* else. Nothing for me could replace what I'm doing right now. *Nothing*!

I saw in my dad *unbelievable* joy. Seeing people saved from sin. Seeing believers surrender their all to the power of the Holy Spirit. Seeing addictions broken, families restored, prodigals come home, marriages healed. The move and work of God never ceases to amaze me, and I know it is what fueled my dad. He preached it, lived it and saw it happen in people's lives again and again.

I saw *unbelievable* friendships. The closest friends my dad has are from following the call of God. There are men in my dad's life from decades ago that still mean the world to him. There will be an amazing reunion in Heaven of the friendships born out of the call.

I saw *unbelievable* peace. The center of God's will is not always the safest place to be, but it is always the *best* place to be! If my dad didn't have peace, he hid it well. Watching as a little boy, a young man and a grown adult, it sure seems he's had peace in the midst of chaos in his life. I think that's due to knowing he was following the call of God and in the center of His will.

I saw an *unbelievable* God. God was real to my dad. My dad believed in what God could do. He believed in an *unbelievable* God. He knew that somehow and some way God would work it all out, regardless of what He was asking our family to do or where He was asking us to go.

I can truly say as one of my dad's three children that we are able to follow him as he follows Christ. I hope my children can say the same thing about me some day. My dad's example to us of what it means to follow the call of God, I believe, will span generations.

Growing up, I lived with my hero. I want my family to live with theirs, and I want your family to live with theirs too! If you take them seriously, these three words will change your life forever...because you're called!

Notes

Chapter 1: What is a calling?

1. "Calling." Def. 1 & 2. *New Oxford American Dictionary 3rd edition* © 2010 by Oxford University Press, Inc.

Chapter 2: Mr. Potato Head Christianity

1. Cruise, Tom, *A Few Good Men.* Rob Reiner. Castle Rock Entertainment, 1992. Film.

Chapter 3: Jesus' Bride, not my back up plan

1. "Bio of Blake Mycoskie, The Founder & Chief Shoe Giver of TOMS Shoes." *TOMS.com.* TOMS Shoes, 2006. Web.
2. "Kiva (Organization)." *Wikipedia*®. Wikimedia Foundation, Inc., July 2013. Web.
3. Davis, Katie. *Kisses from Katie.* Amazima Ministries. 2 November 2010. Web. 1 September 2013.
4. *Amazima.org/katiesbook.* Amazima Ministries, n.d. Web. Aug. 2013.
5. Mowery, Derek. Personal written testimony. August 1, 2013.
6. Doolin, Steve. Personal written testimony. August 1, 2013.

Chapter 4: Faith and Foreskin

1. Big Idea Entertainment (Production Co.). 1997. *Veggie Tales: Josh and the Big Wall!* [DVD]. USA. Phil Vischer & Mike Nawrocki.

Chapter 5: How do I KNOW I'm called?

1. Morgan, Dan. Senior Pastor, High Plains Community Church, Gillette, WY. Personal Communications. Fall, 2004.

2. Hackman, Gene, (Coach) Norman Dale. *Hoosiers.* Dir. David Anspaugh. Orion Pictures, 1986. DVD.

Chapter 7: Inception

1. *Inception.* Dir. Christopher Nolan. Warner Bros. Pictures, 2010. DVD.
2. McManus, Erwin R., *The Barbarian Way: Unleash the Untamed Faith Within.* Nashville: Thomas Nelson, Inc. 2005. Print.
3. *The One Year™ Chronological Bible* copyright ©, Wheaton, Illinois: Tyndale House Publishers, Inc, 2000. Print.

Chapter 8: The cost of the call

1. Matt Redman. "Blessed Be Your Name." *Blessed Be Your NHame the Songs of Matt Redman Vol. 1.* Nathan Nockels, 2005. Radio

About the Author

Jeff Maness is the founding and Lead Pastor of Element Church in Cheyenne, Wyoming. Element started in October of 2007, and is now a multi-site church averaging over 1,200 people each weekend and has a vision to plant campuses throughout the state of Wyoming. The church has been named one of the Fastest Growing Churches in North America by Outreach Magazine. Jeff is a gifted communicator and teacher who strives to speak the truth of God's word as plainly as possible. God has given Jeff a vision and a passion for helping people experience life to its fullest in Christ. Jeff attended and graduated from Oklahoma Wesleyan University in Bartlesville, OK, in 1997, with a degree in Pastoral Ministry. Jeff, his wife Sabrina and their 4 children (Jonah, Mariah, Makalah and Jaydah) live in Cheyenne, Wyoming.

To contact Jeff for speaking at an event or coaching availability, please visit www.jeffmaness.com.

Follow Jeff on Twitter: jeffgmaness
Follow Jeff on Facebook: www.facebook.com/pages/Jeff-Maness/459165947506095

To learn more about Element Church and what God is doing through their ministry, please visit www.elementchurchwy.com.

Salvation Next Steps

Salvation: You just read from John 3:16, "For God so loved the world that he gave his one and only Son, that whoever believes in him shall not perish but have eternal life."

In John 3:3, Jesus called this being "born again". What does it really mean to be born again and *why* should I be born again?

Romans 3:23 tells us, "For everyone has sinned; we all fall short of God's glorious standard." Romans 6:23 teaches us that because of our sin, we are separated from a holy God. We are spiritually dead! "For the wages of sin is death, but the free gift of God is eternal life through Christ Jesus our Lord."

That's *why* we need to be born again, because we are spiritually dead from our sin. So *how* can I be born again?

1. Hear

Romans 10:14
But how can they call on him to save them unless they believe in him? And how can they believe in him if they have never heard about him? And how can they hear about him unless someone tells them?

2. Repent

Repent simply means "to turn". That you're turning from your former life so you can live a new life in God.

Acts 3:19
Now repent of your sins and turn to God, so that your sins may be wiped away.

Corinthians 7:10
or the kind of sorrow God wants us to experience leads us away rom sin and results in salvation. There's no regret for that kind of sorrow. But worldly sorrow, which lacks repentance, results in spiritual death.

3. Confess

1 John 1:9
But if we confess our sins to him, he is faithful and just to forgive us our sins and to cleanse us from all wickedness.

It's not about making a list of all the sins you've ever committed. That would take a while for all of us right? It's about confessing that you are a sinner in need of a Savior, and that Savior is only Jesus.

4. Believe

Romans 10:9
If you confess with your mouth that Jesus is Lord and believe in your heart that God raised him from the dead, you will be saved.

5. Receive

Revelation 3:20
Look! I stand at the door and knock. If you hear my voice and open the door, I will come in, and we will share a meal together as friends.

If you're ready to nail this issue down in your heart, you can do that right now. Below is a prayer you can pray to ask God to do what He promised in His Word He would do. There is nothing magical about this prayer. This is you talking to God:

Father in Heaven, thank you for loving me so much You sent Jesus to die in my place. I believe in Jesus. I believe He died for me, and rose from the dead so He can live in me. Because of that, I confess to you that I am a sinner in need of a Savior. Forgive me of all my sins. I turn from my former way of living, and ask you to help me live a new life. I receive from you salvation. Thank you for loving me and I'll do my best to love you back. In Jesus name, Amen!

If you prayed that prayer we are *so* proud of you, and your Heavenly Father is as well. We'd also love to know about your decision.

Please email us you're story to info@becauseyourecalled.com.